Mastering QuickBooks 2020

The ultimate guide to bookkeeping and QuickBooks Online

Crystalynn Shelton, CPA

BIRMINGHAM - MUMBAI

Mastering QuickBooks 2020

Copyright © 2019 Packt Publishing

All rights reserved. No part of this book may be reproduced, stored in a retrieval system, or transmitted in any form or by any means, without the prior written permission of the publisher, except in the case of brief quotations embedded in critical articles or reviews.

Every effort has been made in the preparation of this book to ensure the accuracy of the information presented. However, the information contained in this book is sold without warranty, either express or implied. Neither the author, nor Packt Publishing or its dealers and distributors, will be held liable for any damages caused or alleged to have been caused directly or indirectly by this book.

Packt Publishing has endeavored to provide trademark information about all of the companies and products mentioned in this book by the appropriate use of capitals. However, Packt Publishing cannot guarantee the accuracy of this information.

Commissioning Editor: Pavan Ramchandani
Acquisition Editor: Karan Gupta
Content Development Editor: Aamir Ahmed
Senior Editor: Hayden Edwards
Technical Editor: Jinesh Topiwala
Copy Editor: Safis Editing
Project Coordinator: Kinjal Bari
Proofreader: Safis Editing
Indexer: Pratik Shirodkar
Production Designer: Aparna Bhagat

First published: December 2019

Production reference: 2070520

Published by Packt Publishing Ltd.
Livery Place
35 Livery Street
Birmingham
B3 2PB, UK.

ISBN 978-1-78995-510-1

www.packt.com

To my mother, Mary A. Moore, who exemplifies the Golden Rule:
Do unto others as you would have them do unto you.
To my husband, Charles, for always being loving and supportive
throughout our joint life journey.

To my fellow accountants, bookkeepers, and tax professionals who spend countless hours
doing their part to help small businesses succeed – I salute you.

– Crystalynn Shelton, CPA

Packt.com

Subscribe to our online digital library for full access to over 7,000 books and videos, as well as industry leading tools to help you plan your personal development and advance your career. For more information, please visit our website.

Why subscribe?

- Spend less time learning and more time coding with practical eBooks and Videos from over 4,000 industry professionals

- Improve your learning with Skill Plans built especially for you

- Get a free eBook or video every month

- Fully searchable for easy access to vital information

- Copy and paste, print, and bookmark content

Did you know that Packt offers eBook versions of every book published, with PDF and ePub files available? You can upgrade to the eBook version at www.packt.com and as a print book customer, you are entitled to a discount on the eBook copy. Get in touch with us at customercare@packtpub.com for more details.

At www.packt.com, you can also read a collection of free technical articles, sign up for a range of free newsletters, and receive exclusive discounts and offers on Packt books and eBooks.

Contributors

About the author

Crystalynn Shelton is a licensed CPA in California. She earned an accounting degree from the University of Texas, Arlington, and has held numerous management roles in the oil and gas, entertainment, education, and retail grocery industries. She ran her own bookkeeping practice for 3 years and worked for Intuit (QuickBooks) for 3 years as a senior learning specialist. Crystalynn is currently a content strategist for Technical Learning Resources and an Adjunct Instructor at UCLA Extension, where she teaches accounting, bookkeeping, and QuickBooks to hundreds of small business owners and accounting students each year. Crystalynn is also an Advanced certified QuickBooks Online ProAdvisor and has been certified in QuickBooks for more than 10 years. When she is not working, Crystalynn enjoys reading a good book and rollerblading in Venice Beach, California.

To the editors, proofreaders, and technical writers at Packt, thank you for all of your hard work to help make this book possible.

To the folks at FitSmallBusiness.com for your part in making me the writer I am today.

About the reviewer

Steven A. Windsor is a chartered certified accountant with almost 20 years' experience and currently works as a business advisory manager for Pascoe Partners Accountants in West Perth, Western Australia, helping small-to-medium businesses grow and meet the dreams and goals of their owners.

He is a big fan of QuickBooks, which he has been using for approximately 18 years (both the desktop and online versions), and has completed the QuickBooks Online Advanced Certification course. Steven is passionate about training people in bookkeeping and finds QuickBooks Online to be one of the most intuitive cloud software packages available.

This is Steven's first book review and he hopes readers will find it as useful and informative as he did.

Ryan Blair is a graduate of the Business Administration-Accounting program at St. Lawrence College in Kingston, Ontario, Canada. He is currently a QuickBooks ProAdvisor, helping small businesses with their bookkeeping needs, as well as offering audit, advisory, and tax services. Ryan has many years of experience in the food and beverage industry and uses that knowledge of operations with his accounting expertise to help clients who are part of that sector. Ryan enjoys reading about different areas of accounting and finance, such as investments, to broaden his knowledge of his field. He is a strong supporter of continuous education and is pursuing advanced certifications in accounting and finance.

Packt is searching for authors like you

If you're interested in becoming an author for Packt, please visit authors.packtpub.com and apply today. We have worked with thousands of developers and tech professionals, just like you, to help them share their insight with the global tech community. You can make a general application, apply for a specific hot topic that we are recruiting an author for, or submit your own idea.

Table of Contents

Preface

Intuit QuickBooks is an accounting software package that helps small business owners manage all their bookkeeping tasks. Its complete range of accounting capabilities, such as tracking income and expenses, managing payroll, simplifying taxes, and accepting online payments, makes QuickBooks software a must-have for business owners and aspiring bookkeepers.

The purpose of this book is to teach small business owners, bookkeepers, and aspiring accountants how to properly use QuickBooks Online. Using a fictitious company, we will demonstrate how to create a QuickBooks Online account; customize key settings for a business; manage customers, vendors, and products and services; enter transactions; generate reports; close the books at the end of the period. QuickBooks records the debits and credits for you so that you don't have to know accounting. However, we will show you what's happening behind the scenes in QuickBooks so that you can understand how your actions in QuickBooks impact financial statements. We will also provide you with tips, shortcuts, and best practices to help you save time and become a QuickBooks pro.

Who this book is for

If you're a small business owner, bookkeeper, or accounting student who wants to learn how to make the most of QuickBooks Online, this book is for you. Business analysts, data analysts, managers, professionals working in bookkeeping, and QuickBooks accountants will also find this guide useful. No experience with QuickBooks Online is required to get started; however, some bookkeeping knowledge will be helpful.

What this book covers

Chapter 1, *Getting Started with QuickBooks Online*, starts off with a brief description of QuickBooks Online, then it gives us more information about the different editions, different versions, and finally how to decide which version is suitable for your business.

Chapter 2, *Company File Setup*, shows how you can set up a QuickBooks Online account for your company and takes you through different options available on the dashboard, followed by what information needs to be added for your company.

Chapter 3, *Migrating to QuickBooks Online*, gives you all the information required for migrating to QuickBooks Online from platforms such as Excel, QuickBooks Desktop, or the data stored on your desktop.

Chapter 4, *Customizing QuickBooks for your Business*, introduces customization for the chart of accounts and then dives into the different ways of connecting bank accounts and credit cards to your QuickBooks Online account, followed by granting users access to your QuickBooks data.

Chapter 5, *Managing Customers, Vendors, Products and Services*, gives you a detailed insight on how to manage your customers, vendors, and products and services.

Chapter 6, *Recording Sales Transactions in QuickBooks Online*, starts by giving detailed information on different forms of sales, followed by how the customer can record payments using different methods, and finally teaches you how to initiate refunds for your customers.

Chapter 7, *Recording Expenses in QuickBooks Online*, teaches you how to enter and pay bills for your QuickBooks Online account. Then we start exploring how to manage recurring expenses, followed by writing and printing checks.

Chapter 8, *Managing Downloaded Bank and Credit Card Transactions*, gives you a brief overview of the banking center in QuickBooks Online and gives you a deep understanding of how the bank rules work, followed by how to edit QuickBooks Online transactions, and finally how to reconcile bank accounts.

Chapter 9, *Report Center Overview*, takes you through the report center, followed by the different reports available, how to customize and export reports, and finally how to send reports via email.

Chapter 10, *Business Overview Reports*, discusses the three primary reports that provide a good overview of your business: the profit and loss statement, balance sheet report, and statement of cash flows.

Chapter 11, *Customer Sales Reports in QuickBooks Online*, focuses on reports that will give you insight into your customers and sales. We will discuss what information you will find on each report, how to customize the reports, and how to generate each report.

Chapter 12, *Vendor and Expenses Reports*, dives into what information you can expect to find on each report, how to customize the report, and how to generate it. This chapter also discusses ways that you can use the report to help you manage your expenses and cash flow.

Chapter 13, *Managing Payroll in QuickBooks Online*, shows you how to set up your payroll system, how to generate payroll, and how to fill payroll tax forms and payments.

Chapter 14, *Managing 1099 Contractors in QuickBooks Online*, shows you how to set up 1099 contractors, tracking and paying 1099 contractors, followed by how to generate the 1099 year ending report.

Chapter 15, *Closing the Books in QuickBooks Online*, covers reconciling all bank and credit card accounts, making year-end accrual adjustments (if applicable), recording fixed asset purchases made throughout the year, recording depreciation, taking a physical inventory, adjusting retained earnings, and preparing financial statements.

Chapter 16, *Handling Special Transactions in QuickBooks Online*, starts by using apps in QuickBooks Online. Apps are a great way to help you streamline day-to-day business tasks that can be time-consuming. Next, we will show you how to record credit card payments from customers. We will also show you how to keep track of petty cash. Finally, we will show you how to record delayed charges.

To get the most out of this book

This book is ideal for anyone who has accounting/bookkeeping knowledge as well as those that don't. Each chapter builds on the knowledge and information presented in the previous chapters. If you don't have any experience of using QuickBooks Online, we recommend you start with Chapter 1, *Getting Started with QuickBooks Online*, and complete each chapter in the order it is presented. If you have experience of using QuickBooks Online, feel free to advance to the chapters that cover the topics you need to brush up on.

Download the example code files

You can download the example code files for this book from your account at www.packt.com. If you purchased this book elsewhere, you can visit www.packtpub.com/support and register to have the files emailed directly to you.

You can download the code files by following these steps:

1. Log in or register at www.packt.com.
2. Select the **Support** tab.
3. Click on **Code Downloads**.
4. Enter the name of the book in the **Search** box and follow the onscreen instructions.

Once the file is downloaded, please make sure that you unzip or extract the folder using the latest version of:

- WinRAR/7-Zip for Windows
- Zipeg/iZip/UnRarX for Mac
- 7-Zip/PeaZip for Linux

We also have other code bundles from our rich catalog of books and videos available at https://github.com/PacktPublishing/. Check them out!

Conventions used

Bold: Indicates a new term, an important word, or words that you see on screen. For example, words in menus or dialog boxes appear in the text like this. Here is an example: "Click on the **Accounting** tab located on the left menu bar and select **Chart of Accounts**."

Warnings or important notes appear like this.

Tips and tricks appear like this.

Get in touch

Feedback from our readers is always welcome.

General feedback: If you have questions about any aspect of this book, mention the book title in the subject of your message and email us at customercare@packtpub.com.

Errata: Although we have taken every care to ensure the accuracy of our content, mistakes do happen. If you have found a mistake in this book, we would be grateful if you would report this to us. Please visit www.packtpub.com/support/errata, selecting your book, clicking on the Errata Submission Form link, and entering the details.

Piracy: If you come across any illegal copies of our works in any form on the Internet, we would be grateful if you would provide us with the location address or website name. Please contact us at copyright@packt.com with a link to the material.

If you are interested in becoming an author: If there is a topic that you have expertise in and you are interested in either writing or contributing to a book, please visit authors.packtpub.com.

Reviews

Please leave a review. Once you have read and used this book, why not leave a review on the site that you purchased it from? Potential readers can then see and use your unbiased opinion to make purchase decisions, we at Packt can understand what you think about our products, and our authors can see your feedback on their book. Thank you!

For more information about Packt, please visit packt.com.

1
Getting Started with QuickBooks Online

Before diving into the nuts and bolts of setting up QuickBooks for your business, you should understand what QuickBooks is, and what your options are when it comes to using it. Once you know what your options are, you will be in a better position to choose the version of QuickBooks that will best suit your business needs.

If you don't have previous experience as a bookkeeper, then you will need to know a few bookkeeping basics before you get started. In the introduction to the bookkeeping section, we cover five key areas in terms of recording transactions in your business: money coming in, money going out, inventory purchases, fixed asset purchases, and liabilities. In this section, we will also cover the importance of the chart of accounts, accounting methods, and what double-entry bookkeeping is.

We will cover the following key concepts in this chapter:

- What is QuickBooks?
- **QuickBooks Online (QBO)** editions
- Choosing the right QBO edition
- **QuickBooks Desktop (QBD)** product line
- Choosing the right QBD version
- New features in QBD 2019 and 2020
- Introduction to small business bookkeeping

Once you've got these key concepts under your belt, you will be ready to dive into setting up your business in QBO.

What is QuickBooks?

QuickBooks is an accounting software program that allows you to track your business' income and expenses. One of the benefits of using QuickBooks is having access to key financial reports (such as profit and loss) so that you can see the overall health of your business at any time. Having access to these reports makes filing your taxes a breeze. QuickBooks has been around for almost three decades, and it is the accounting software used by millions of small businesses around the globe.

QuickBooks comes in two formats: a software that you can install or download on a desktop computer, and a cloud-based program that you can access from any mobile device or desktop computer with an internet connection.

The cloud-based version, **QuickBooks Online (QBO)**, is available in four editions: Simple Start, Essentials, Plus, and Advanced. The desktop version, **QuickBooks Desktop (QBD)**, also comes in four editions: QuickBooks Mac, Pro, Premier, and Enterprise. We will discuss each of these in detail next.

QBO editions

QBO comes in four editions:

- Simple Start
- Essentials
- Plus
- Advanced

Each edition varies in terms of the price, the number of users to which you can give access, and the features included.

The following table gives a summary of QBO pricing and features, in each edition of QBO:

	QBO Simple Start	QBO Essentials	QBO Plus	QBO Advanced
Monthly cost	$20	$35	$60	$150
Track income and expenses	✓	✓	✓	✓
Connect bank and credit card accounts	✓	✓	✓	✓
Manage accounts receivable	✓	✓	✓	✓
Accept online payments	✓	✓	✓	✓
Send estimates	✓	✓	✓	✓
Track sales tax	✓	✓	✓	✓

Manage accounts payable		✓	✓	✓
Maximum number of users (includes two accountant users)	3	5	7	25
Time tracking		✓	✓	✓
Track project profitability			✓	✓
Inventory tracking			✓	✓
Track payments to 1099 contractors			✓	✓
Dedicated customer success manager				✓
QuickBooks training for staff				✓
Smart Reporting with Fathom				✓
Import customer invoices				✓
Custom user permissions				✓

As you can see from the preceding table, all four editions of QBO include the following features:

- **Track income and expenses**: Keep track of all sales to customers and expenses paid to vendors.
- **Connect bank and credit card accounts**: Connect all business bank and credit cards to QBO so transactions automatically download into the software.
- **Manage accounts receivable**: Invoice customers, enter payments, and stay on top of unpaid invoices.
- **Accept online payments**: Allow customers to pay their invoices online with debit/credit card or by wire transfer.
- **Send estimates**: Create a quote or proposal, and email it to prospective clients for approval.
- **Track sales tax**: Keep track of sales tax collected from customers, submit electronic payments to state and local authorities, and complete required sales tax forms and filings.
- **Maximum number of users**: Each plan includes two accountant users, plus one or more additional users. For example, you can give a bookkeeper and your **certified public accountant (CPA)** access to your data.

The Simple Start plan is the most economical, at $20 per month. It includes one user and two accountants. The Essentials plan is the next tier and starts at $35 per month. It includes three users and two accountants. Unlike Simple Start, you can track **accounts payable (A/P)** with the Essentials plan. The Plus plan is $60 per month. It includes five users and two accountants. Unlike the Simple Start and Essentials plans, you can track your inventory with the Plus plan. The Advanced plan is the top-tier QBO plan. It starts at $150 per month, and includes up to 25 users.

We will discuss the features of each plan in more detail, and how to choose the right QBO version for you, in the next section.

Choosing the right QBO edition

QBO is ideal for solopreneurs, freelancers, and mid-to-large-sized businesses with employees and 1099 contractors. 1099 contractors are also known as independent contractors, who you may hire to provide services for your business. Since they are not employees of the business, you must provide a 1099 form at the end of the year to any contractor you have paid $600 or more to in the calendar year.

The needs of your business will determine which edition of QBO is ideal for you. The following provides some additional insight into the ideal businesses for each edition of QBO.

QBO Simple Start

QBO Simple Start is ideal for a freelancer or sole proprietor that sells services only, and no products. You may have employees that you need to pay, but you don't have any 1099 contractors. The majority of your expenses are paid via online banking or wire transfer, so you don't need to write or print checks to pay bills.

QBO Essentials

Similar to QBO Simple Start, QBO Essentials is ideal for freelancers and sole proprietors that only sell services only, and no products. You have employees but you do not hire contractors. Unlike QBO Simple Start, you pay most of your bills by writing checks, and you need the ability to keep track of your unpaid bills, also referred to as A/P.

QBO Plus

Unlike QBO Simple Start and QBO Essentials, QBO Plus is ideal for small businesses that sell products, since it includes inventory tracking. Similar to QBO Simple Start and QBO Essentials, you can pay employees. QBO Plus also allows you to keep track of payments made to 1099 contractors so that you can complete the required 1099 reporting at the end of the year.

QBO Advanced

QBO Advanced is ideal for businesses that have more than five users needing access to their data. QBO Advanced is QBO Plus on steroids: it includes all of the features found in QBO Plus, along with some great bonus features, such as training for your entire team, and Smart Reporting with Fathom.

The bonus features that you will find in QBO Advanced are as follows:

- **Dedicated customer success manager**: With a QBO Advanced subscription, you are assigned a point of contact, who will learn how your business works in order to answer your questions. They will also provide additional resources that will help you to better manage your business financials.
- **QuickBooks training for staff**: With QBO Advanced, you get $2,000 worth of self-paced training materials and resources, to help you and your team get up to speed on how to use QBO.
- **Smart Reporting with Fathom**: With this reporting feature, you can measure profitability, cash flow, and other **key performance indicators** (**KPIs**). This feature is not available in any other QBO edition.
- **Import customer invoices**: Allows you to eliminate manually creating invoices one by one. Instead, you can import and email hundreds of invoices, all at once.
- **Custom user permissions**: Provides a deeper level of user permissions that allows you to manage access to sensitive data, such as bank accounts.

Depending on your business and individual circumstances, you should now be able to determine whether you will need QBO Simple Start, Essentials, Plus, or Advanced. It is important to pick the right version for you so that you have access to the appropriate features you will need. Next, we will provide a brief overview of the QBD product line.

QBD product line

QBD comes in four editions:

- Mac
- Pro
- Premier
- Enterprise

Each edition varies in terms of the price, the number of users to which you can give access, and the features included.

The following table provides a summary of the cost and features included in each edition of QBD:

	QuickBooks for Mac	QuickBooks Pro	QuickBooks Premier	QuickBooks Enterprise
Cost	$299.95	$299.95	$499.95	$1,155/year*
Track income and expenses	✓	✓	✓	✓
Connect bank and credit card accounts	✓	✓	✓	✓
Manage accounts receivable	✓	✓	✓	✓
Manage accounts payable	✓	✓	✓	✓
Accept online payments	✓	✓	✓	✓
Number of financial reports included	100+	100+	150+ industry-specific	150+ advanced reporting
Send estimates	✓	✓	✓	✓
Track sales tax	✓	✓	✓	✓
Maximum number of users	3	3	5	30
Time tracking	✓	✓	✓	✓
Inventory tracking	✓	✓	✓	✓
Pay 1099 contractors	✓	✓	✓	✓
Create budgets/forecasting	✓		✓	✓
Industry-specific features			✓	✓
Mobile inventory barcode scanning				✓
Enhanced Pick, Pack, and Ship				✓

 QuickBooks Enterprise has an annual subscription.

As you can see from the preceding table, all four editions of QBD include the following features:

- **Track income and expenses**: Keep track of all sales to customers and expenses paid to vendor suppliers.
- **Connect bank and credit card accounts**: Connect all business bank and credit cards to QBO so transactions automatically download into the software.

- **Manage accounts receivable**: Invoice customers, enter payments, and stay on top of unpaid invoices.
- **Manage accounts payable**: Track unpaid bills, and pay them by check or through online banking before they are due.
- **Accept online payments**: Allow customers to pay their invoices online with debit/credit card, or through **Automated Clearing House (ACH)**.
- **Send estimates**: Create a quote or proposal, and email it to prospective clients for approval.
- **Track sales tax**: Keep track of sales tax collected from customers, submit electronic payments to state and local authorities, and complete required state tax forms and filings.
- **Give other users access**: Give other users—such as a bookkeeper or an accountant—access to your data.
- **Time tracking**: Track hours worked by employees and contractors, so you can easily bill customers for completed work.
- **Inventory tracking**: Track inventory costs and quantities, using the average cost inventory method.
- **Pay 1099 contractors**: Keep track of payments made to independent contractors, and file the required tax forms at the end of the year.

QuickBooks Mac and Pro versions are priced at $299.95 and are identical when it comes to features included. If your business falls into one of five industries (nonprofit, manufacturing and wholesale, professional services, contractor, or retail), you should choose QuickBooks Premier, which starts at $499.95. Finally, if your business has extensive inventory requirements, QuickBooks Enterprise includes mobile inventory barcode scanning and the Enhanced Pick, Pack, and Shipping feature that none of the other editions offer.

You now have a better understanding of the QBD product line. This information will go a long way to help you determine which desktop version is right for your business. In the next section, we will go into more detail about what is included in the four QBD versions.

Choosing the right QBD version

QBD is ideal for small-to-large-sized businesses that sell products or services, have employees and contractors, and are looking for a robust desktop accounting solution. If you have a Mac, QuickBooks for Mac is going to work best for you. For small businesses that use a PC or a Windows computer, you've got three versions to choose from: QuickBooks Pro, Premier, or Enterprise. Let's look at these in more detail.

QuickBooks Mac

QuickBooks Mac is ideal for any sized business on an iOS platform that has less than $1 million in annual revenue and doesn't need to give more than three users access to QuickBooks. When it comes to the features included, QuickBooks Mac is almost identical to QuickBooks Pro. You can connect your bank accounts, invoice customers, and pay bills, just like you can in the Pro, Premier, and Enterprise versions. Unfortunately, QuickBooks Mac does not come in industry-specific versions, unlike QuickBooks Premier and Enterprise.

For 2019, QuickBooks Mac has added a couple of new features that you won't find in QuickBooks Pro, Premier, or Enterprise: iCloud Document Sharing, and the ability to import your sales from Square. Square is a mobile payment company that allows small businesses to accept credit card payments from customers.

Here is some further information about what is included in QuickBooks Mac 2019:

- **iCloud document sharing**: Share files between multiple Macs connected through iCloud.
- **Reconciliation discrepancy report**: This report allows you to identify reconciliation discrepancies between bank statements and QuickBooks.
- **Customer and vendor center email tracking**: Emails sent directly from QuickBooks to vendors and customers will be logged in the *Emails* section of the vendor and customer centers.
- **Past due stamps**: A *past due* stamp will now appear on delinquent invoices, so when you print or email them to customers in order to expedite payments, the stamp will immediately alert the customer that their payment is past the due date, which should prompt them to make a payment.
- **Square import**: If you use Square to track your sales, you can easily import that data into QuickBooks Mac.

QuickBooks Pro

QuickBooks Pro is ideal for a business of any size that is on a Windows platform, has less than $1 million in annual revenue, and does not need more than three user licenses. It includes all of the features found in QuickBooks Mac, plus it includes more than 100 customizable reports. You can also track hours worked by employees and contractors, to bill back customers as work is completed. Unfortunately, QuickBooks Pro does not come in industry-specific versions, unlike the QuickBooks Premier and Enterprise versions.

QuickBooks Premier

QuickBooks Premier is ideal for small-to-medium-sized businesses that fall into one of the following industries:

- Nonprofit
- Manufacturing and wholesale
- Professional services
- Contractor
- Retail

Unlike QuickBooks Mac and Pro, QuickBooks Premier includes a customized chart of accounts, a custom products and services list, and reports customized for businesses that fall into the industries listed previously. QuickBooks Premier also allows you to purchase up to five user licenses, and it includes a forecasting tool.

QuickBooks Enterprise

QuickBooks Enterprise is the top-tier QBD plan. It includes all of the features you will find in QuickBooks Premier, plus a number of bonus ones.

QuickBooks Enterprise includes the following additional features:

- **Up to 30 user licenses**: You can purchase up to a maximum of 30 user licenses for multiuser access.
- **Granular user access permissions**: Includes more restrictive user permissions than other versions of QuickBooks.
- **Mobile inventory barcode scanning**: Prioritizes sales orders to fulfill, creates customer picklists across multiple warehouses, and sends this information to a barcode scanner.
- **Enhanced Pick, Pack, and Ship**: Sends items to a picker or packer, with just one click. Plus, you can fill out and print shipping labels for major carriers, directly from QuickBooks.

You should now have a better understanding of the differences between QuickBooks Mac, Pro, Premier, and Enterprise. This information should help you decide which desktop edition is right for your business. In the next section, we will provide details on the new features available in QBD.

New features in QBD 2019 and 2020

Each year, there are improvements and new features added to the QBD product line. Here is a summary of the new features available in QBD 2019 and 2020.

New features in QBD 2019

The new 2019 QBD features included in QuickBooks Pro, Premier, and Enterprise are as follows:

- **Customer invoice history tracker**: Real-time invoice status tracking, so you can take action to communicate with customers about unpaid invoices. Invoice creation date, due date, viewed date, and email date are just a few of the statuses.
- **Condensed data file optimization**: This feature reduces the size of your QuickBooks company file, without deleting data. QuickBooks also cleans up performance logs and other details that could result in up to a 32% file size reduction.
- **Easy upgrades**: It is a simple two-click process to install the latest version of QBD. The upgrade process has been completely automated, and you will be given the option to retain the older version of QuickBooks.

New features in QBD 2020

The new QBD 2020 features included in QuickBooks Pro, Premier and Enterprise are as follows:

- **Automated payment reminders:** A feature that has been included in QuickBooks Online for a few years now, and is also available in QBD 2020. You can now schedule, review, and send payment reminders to customers for past due invoices or for invoices that are due soon.
- **Automatically add customer purchase order number to invoice emails**: To help customers quickly identify the items on an open invoice, QBD includes an invoice email template that includes the purchase order number in the subject line of the email.
- **Combine multiple emails:** Another new feature included in QBD 2020 is the ability to combine multiple invoices into one email. Instead of sending a customer one email for each outstanding invoice, you can attach all open invoices for a single customer in one email.

- **Company file search:** Quickly locate a company file by using the new file search option located on the **No Company Open** screen.
- **Easier admin password reset:** The new version of QuickBooks makes it a lot easier to reset the admin password for your company file. From a drop-down menu, select an email address from a list of emails registered with QuickBooks, enter a token you will receive via email, and your password will be reset.
- **Enhanced accessibility**: Improved usability for visually-challenged users on the **Bills, Invoice**, and **Write Checks** screens.
- **Collapse columns in reports**: When viewing reports, you can now collapse columns (such as jobs and classes) to view customer totals or class totals without scrolling or exporting to Excel..
- **Payroll status for direct deposit-enabled customers**: You can check the status of a direct deposit payroll run directly in QuickBooks, without having to check emails or call tech support.
- **Smart Help**: Press *F1* for improved content and a better search experience, or access care agents through messaging and callback options.

Now that we have a better understanding of the features included in the QBO and the QBD product lines, we're going to dive into a few bookkeeping basics. While you don't need an accounting degree or a bookkeeping background to use QuickBooks, you should be familiar with some basic bookkeeping terminology and key concepts.

Introduction to small business bookkeeping

If you are an aspiring accountant, the concepts that we will cover in this section will be familiar to you. However, if you are brand new to bookkeeping, make sure you grab a notepad to take notes, and a cup of coffee to stay alert. In this section, we will discuss the following: money coming into your business; money going out of your business; inventory and fixed asset purchases; the money you owe (liabilities); how to properly track everything using the chart of accounts; the two accounting methods; and double-entry bookkeeping.

One of the benefits of using QuickBooks to manage your books is that you don't need an accounting degree to learn how to use the software. However, you should have a basic understanding of how bookkeeping works and of what's happening behind the scenes in QuickBooks when you record transactions. As we walk through how to record transactions in QuickBooks, we will also explain what is happening behind the scenes, to further deepen your understanding of bookkeeping.

The main areas of your business include the following:

- Money in (sales)
- Money out (expenses)
- Inventory and fixed asset purchases
- Liabilities
- Chart of accounts
- Accounting methods
- Double-entry bookkeeping

Let's discuss each of these areas in more detail.

Money in (sales)

Every business generates sales by either selling products, services, or a combination of the two. For example, a freelance photographer provides photography services for weddings, graduations, and other special events. A retailer that sells custom T-shirts in various sizes and colors provides a product to generate sales.

In general, there are two types of sales: cash sales and credit sales. The primary difference between the two is in terms of when you receive payment from your customer. Cash sales are sales that require payment at the time a product is sold or services have been provided. For example, let's say a customer walks into a T-shirt shop and buys a T-shirt. This sale would be considered a cash sale because the sale of the T-shirt and payment by the customer takes place at the same time.

Credit sales are the opposite of cash sales because the sale and the payment by the customer take place at separate intervals. For example, let's say the freelance photographer spends four hours at a wedding and sends their customer a bill a few days later. This is considered a credit sale because payment will take place sometime in the future after services have been rendered.

For bookkeeping purposes, credit sales are recorded as accounts receivable. Accounts receivable, also referred to as A/R, is the money that is owed to you by customers. We will talk more about how to keep track of your A/R balances later on.

Now that you understand sales, let's take a look at expenses.

Money out (expenses)

The majority of the money that flows out of a business is used to pay for business expenses. Business expenses can be categorized as recurring or non-recurring. A recurring expense is one that repeats, such as rent, utilities, and insurance.

A non-recurring expense is one that is unexpected. For example, if a photographer's camera stops working and they need to spend money to get it repaired or buy a new one, this would be considered a non-recurring expense because it was unexpected.

QuickBooks is designed to help you easily track both recurring and non-recurring expenses. In this book, we will cover how to create recurring transactions in QuickBooks so that you don't have to manually enter them each time they occur. Plus, you will learn how to pay non-recurring transactions by writing a check, making online payments, or paying with a credit or debit card.

Now that you know how to keep track of money coming into your business and money going out of your business, let's see how you should handle inventory and fixed asset purchases next.

Inventory and fixed asset purchases

To keep track of all the costs and quantities for each item that you purchase, you would create a purchase order and send it to your vendor supplier to place an order. When you receive the goods, you would record them in your inventory. As you sell products to customers, you will record the sale in QuickBooks so that your inventory, cost, and quantities can be adjusted in real time.

If you purchase computers, printers, or other equipment for your business, these items are called fixed assets. When you record these items in QuickBooks, they will be categorized as fixed assets. Fixed assets must be depreciated over their useful life.

Liabilities

Many people think that liabilities are expenses, but they are not. A liability can be described as a loan you have with a financial institution, or money that you owe to vendor suppliers, which is also called A/P. The primary difference between expenses and liabilities is that if you were to go out of business tomorrow, you would no longer have to pay expenses. Instead, you would stop making payments for utilities, and you would lay off employees to eliminate payroll expenses.

On the other hand, if you go out of business, you still have to pay your outstanding liabilities. For example, if you have an outstanding loan with a bank, you still have to make your loan payment until it has been paid off. The same would apply for unpaid bills for products and/or services you received. This means you would have to contact the vendor/supplier and notify them you are going out of business in order to make payment arrangements.

Chart of accounts

The chart of accounts is a systematic way of categorizing business financial transactions. Every transaction for your business can be categorized into one of five primary categories: Income, Expenses, Assets, Liabilities, and Owner's Equity.

Here is a brief description of each category, with an example:

- **Income**: Proceeds from the sale of products, such as T-shirts, or services such as photography or consulting services.
- **Expenses**: Payments made to maintain daily business operations. This includes, but is not limited to, rent, utilities, payroll, and office supplies.
- **Assets**: Assets are items that your business owns. For example, the money in your business checking account is an asset, and the inventory that you have on hand is an asset.
- **Liabilities**: As discussed, liabilities consist of money that you owe to creditors. This includes loans, lines of credit, and the money owed to vendor suppliers (for example, A/P).
- **Owner's Equity**: Equity is everything that your business owns. For example, any money that you invest in your business is equity.

When setting up your QuickBooks company, you don't have to worry about creating a chart of accounts from scratch. Instead, QuickBooks will create a default chart of accounts, based on the industry your business falls into.

Accounting methods

One of the key decisions you need to make when setting up your books is which accounting method you will use. There are two accounting methods to choose from: cash-basis accounting, and accrual accounting. The primary difference between the two accounting methods is the point when you record sales and purchase transactions in your books.

Cash-basis accounting involves recording sales and purchases when cash changes hands. Let's say a photographer is not paid right away for most of his jobs, but instead, he sends an invoice to the customer that includes a payment due date. Until the photographer receives payment in cash, or by check or credit card, he does not count the photography services as income under the cash-basis accounting method.

Accrual accounting involves recording sales as soon as you have shipped the products to your customer, or have provided services. Going back to our photographer example, the photographer would count the services he provided as income once he completed taking pictures, regardless of when the customer actually pays for the services.

In general, most small business owners will start out using the cash-basis accounting method. However, according to the **Internal Revenue Service (IRS)**, there are certain types of businesses that are **not** allowed to use this method of accounting.

The following businesses should **never** use cash-basis accounting:

- Businesses that carry an inventory
- C-corporations (regular corporations)
- Businesses with gross annual sales that exceed $5 million

One of the benefits of using QuickBooks is, regardless of which accounting method you choose, it does not change how you record transactions. As a matter of fact, you can start recording transactions into QuickBooks and decide later on which method you will use. As we will discuss in the chapter on reports, you can run reports for either method (cash or accrual).

Double-entry bookkeeping

You may have heard the term double-entry accounting/bookkeeping. This means that, for every financial transaction that you record, there are at least two entries—a debit and a credit. This ensures that both sides of the accounting equation always remain in balance.

The accounting equation is as follows:

Assets = Liabilities + Owner's Equity

Let's look at the following example.

Let's say a T-shirt owner goes out and purchases $100 in T-shirts from a supplier. He doesn't pay for the T-shirts right away, but the supplier will send him a bill later on. For this transaction, inventory increases by $100 and liabilities increase by $100. Since both assets and liabilities increased, our books remain in balance.

The impact of this transaction on the accounting equation is as follows:

```
Assets = Liabilities + Owner's Equity
$100 = $100 + $0
```

Behind the scenes in QuickBooks, the following journal entry would be recorded for this transaction:

Financial Impact	Account	Amount
Debit (Dr.)	Inventory (T-Shirts)	$100
Credit (Cr.)	Accounts Payable	$100

In this section, we have covered the seven main areas of focus for managing the books for your business: money coming into your business in the form of sales to customers; money going out of business for expenses such as office supplies and rent; inventory and fixed asset purchases, and how to record them on your books; money you owe to suppliers and creditors (liabilities); how to manage the chart of accounts; the two accounting methods (cash-basis versus accrual); and how double-entry bookkeeping works.

Summary

In this chapter, we explained what QuickBooks is and introduced you to the QBO and QBD product lines. We also provided tips on how to choose the right software for your business, and we provided you with some bookkeeping basics. Having a good understanding of the QuickBooks product lines will help you to choose the best product for your business. In addition, having a basic knowledge of bookkeeping helps you understand the accounting that is taking place behind the scenes in QuickBooks when you enter an invoice or pay a bill.

In the next chapter, we will take a look at what information you will need to convert from your existing accounting software to QBO. This will include the following: gathering key documents, answering questions about your business needs, and understanding the order you need to follow when bringing over historical data into QuickBooks. If you don't currently use accounting software, we will show you how to set up QuickBooks from scratch.

Company File Setup

2

In this chapter, we will show you how to create a QuickBooks Online account. We will also show you how to navigate in QuickBooks Online. Using the key information and documents we covered in Chapter 1, *Getting Started with QuickBooks Online*, we will walk through the company settings that allow you to establish how you want to record sales, expenses, payments, and other advanced settings such as a fiscal year and which accounting method to use. It's important to include as much information as possible when performing the initial company file setup before you start entering transactions into QuickBooks. Otherwise, you will be missing key information that should appear on customer invoices, documents, and forms that can be produced in QuickBooks.

In this chapter, we'll cover the following topics:

- Creating a QuickBooks Online account
- Navigating in QuickBooks Online
- Setting up company preferences in QuickBooks Online

Creating a QuickBooks Online account

The first step to setting up your business in QuickBooks Online is to create a QuickBooks Online account. To create a QuickBooks Online account, you need to go to the Intuit website and select a QBO subscription plan.

Follow these steps to create a QuickBooks Online account:

1. Open your web browser and go to the Intuit website: `www.intuit.com`.
2. Click on **Products** and select **QuickBooks**, as shown in the following screenshot:

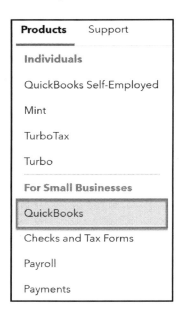

3. Click on **Plans & pricing**, as indicated in the following screenshot:

4. Choose from one of the four pricing plans: **Simple Start**, **Essentials**, **Plus**, and **Advanced**, as indicated in the following screenshot:

5. Create an Intuit account by providing your business email address, mobile number, and password, as indicated in the following screenshot:

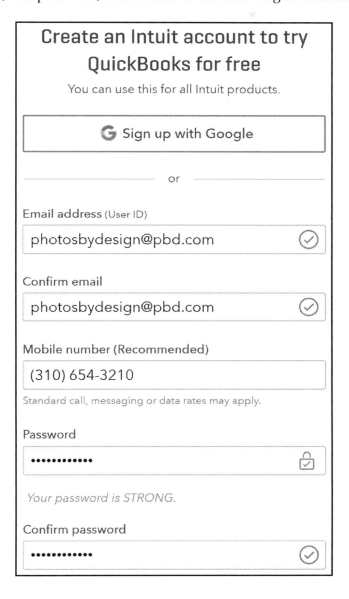

6. Provide your business name, the number of years you've been in business, and specify whether you are converting from QuickBooks Desktop, as indicated in the following screenshot. If you are not currently using QuickBooks Desktop Pro, Premier, or Enterprise, you can just leave the last box blank:

No two businesses are alike

We should know—we've seen a lot! Help us get to know yours.

What's your business called?

Photos By Design

How long have you been in business?

Less than 1 year

☐ I've been using QuickBooks Desktop and want to bring in my data.

Next

7. Click on each task you would like to track in QuickBooks, as indicated in the following screenshot:

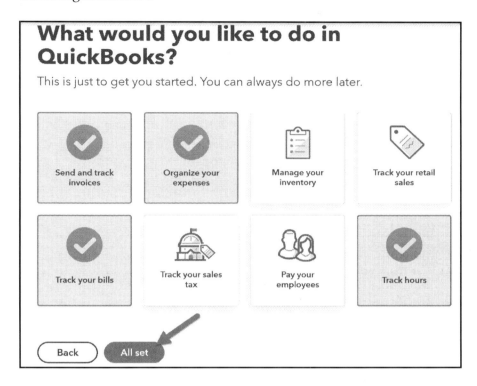

Now that you have created your QuickBooks Online account, you are one step closer to managing your books. Next, we will show you how to navigate through the program, which will help you locate what you need to get your business set up.

Navigating in QuickBooks Online

QuickBooks Online is a very intuitive piece of software. The initial home page is customizable so that you can see key data such as invoices, expenses, profit and loss, bank accounts, and sales. There are a variety of ways you can navigate within the program, including the following:

- Dashboards
- Icons
- Menus (including within the gear icon and the quick create menu).

Let's look at the QuickBooks Online Dashboard first.

The dashboard includes tiles that you can click on to navigate to invoices, expenses, or bank accounts. There are also three menus: the left menu bar, the **Quick Create** menu, and the menu located behind the gear icon.

QuickBooks Online dashboard

To explore what a QuickBooks dashboard will look like, we will use the example of a sample company called Photos By Design:

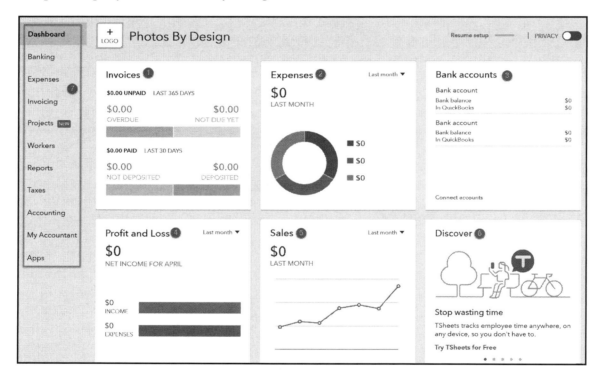

A brief explanation of the information that appears on the QuickBooks Online home page is as follows:

- **Invoices**: In this section, you will see a summary of paid and unpaid customer invoices. Plus, you will see the number of payments that have been received from customers that have been deposited and not deposited. If you click the tile, you can drill down to the specific invoices and deposits that make up the totals that appear there.
- **Expenses**: In this section, you will see a summary of expenses by type (for example, office supplies, bank fees, and so on). You can select the time period you would like to view this information for (for example, monthly, quarterly, or annually) from the dropdown in the upper right corner of the tile.
- **Bank accounts**: A list of all the bank accounts you have connected to QuickBooks Online will appear in this section.

 You can connect bank and credit card accounts to QuickBooks so that your transactions will automatically download for you.

- **Profit and loss**: A snapshot of your total income and expenses will appear in this section. You can select the time period (for example, monthly, quarterly, or annually) you would like to view from the dropdown menu in the upper right-hand corner. Click on the income or expense bar to drill down to the details that make up the totals.
- **Sales**: This tile shows a line graph of how sales are trending for a period of time. You can select the time period from the dropdown menu in the upper right-hand corner.
- **Time tracking**: QuickBooks Online integrates with TSheets. TSheets is a time tracking app that allows you to stay on top of the hours that have been worked by employees, contractors, and owners.
- **Left menu bar**: You can navigate to various areas of QuickBooks Online by using the left menu bar. As shown in the preceding screenshot, you can navigate to other areas of the program such as projects, reports, and workers.

Now that you have a better understanding of the dashboard and how to customize it to fit your needs, let's look at the next navigation tool: icons.

QuickBooks Online icons

The following screenshot shows the common icons that can be found on the QBO home page:

The following are the options you can see in the preceding screenshot:

1. **Quick Create**: This icon will display a menu of tasks that you can perform in QuickBooks Online. Tasks related to customers, vendors, and employees can be found here.
2. **Search**: If you need to locate an invoice, bill, or any transaction, you can do a global search of the program by typing an amount name, the name of a vendor, or any information in this field to search for it.
3. **Gear**: This icon will display a menu of tasks that you can perform in QuickBooks Online. Tasks related to global company settings, lists, and tools such as reconciling and budgeting can be found here.
4. **Help menu**: If you have a question or need to learn how to do something in QBO, you can click on this icon to launch the help menu. You will find detailed support articles, video tutorials, and access to a sample company file in this section.
5. **Notifications**: Notifications about changes that have been made to your account or upgrades to your QuickBooks Online subscription can be found here.

As we mentioned previously, the QBO icons allow you to navigate the program so that you can quickly get to the information you need. In addition to icons, the QBO menus allow you to access your overall company settings, lists, tools, and your company profile. We will cover QuickBooks Online menus next.

QuickBooks Online menus

In addition to the left menu bar, there are a couple more menus you can use to navigate QBO.

The first menu is accessible through the gear icon, located in the upper right-hand corner, to the left of the help icon.

The following screenshot shows the menu that will be displayed when you click on the gear icon:

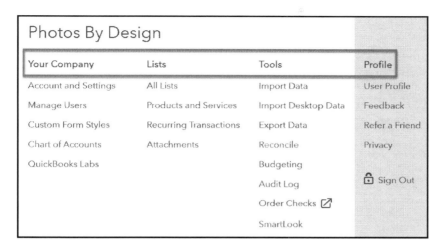

A brief description of the areas of QuickBooks Online that you can access through the gear icon is as follows:

- **Your company**: This section includes global company account settings, which we will explore in detail in the next section. It also allows you to manage users, which is where you can give others access to your QuickBooks data. You can launch the chart of accounts from here and the testing area for new features that are in beta. QuickBooks labs can also be found here.
- **Lists**: The list menu includes all QuickBooks lists, such as customer listing, vendor listing, and products and services listing. Recurring transactions are available here and any files or images that you have attached to QuickBooks transactions, such as receipts or signed contracts, are accessible in the form of attachments.
- **Tools**: The QBO subscription that you have will determine the tools that are listed in this section. We are using the QuickBooks Plus subscription, which includes budgeting and SmartLook. It also provides us with the ability to import data such as banking transactions, customer and vendor lists, chart of accounts, and products and services.
- **Profile**: The profile menu includes a user profile (specific to the user that's currently logged in), a feedback section where you can submit recommendations or issues to the Intuit team, the option to refer a friend, and the built-in privacy features included in QBO.

The second menu that is available in QuickBooks is the Quick Create menu. You can access this menu by clicking on the **Quick Create** icon (plus sign) located to the left of the magnifying glass. The following screenshot shows the menu that you will see when you click on the **Quick Create** icon:

Create

Customers	Vendors	Employees	Other
Invoice	Expense	Payroll	Bank Deposit
Receive Payment	Check	Single Time Activity	Transfer
Estimate	Bill	Weekly Timesheet	Journal Entry
Credit Memo	Pay Bills		Statement
Sales Receipt	Purchase Order		Inventory Qty Adjustment
Refund Receipt	Vendor Credit		
Delayed Credit	Credit Card Credit		
Delayed Charge	Print Checks		

A brief description of the areas of QuickBooks Online that you can access through the **Quick Create** icon are as follows:

- **Customers**: Most of the transactions that pertain to customers can be found here, from creating invoices and sales receipts to accepting customer payments.
- **Vendors**: The tasks related to vendors can be found in this section. This includes recording expenses, writing checks, tracking unpaid bills, and creating purchase orders.
- **Employees**: If you sign up for a QuickBooks payroll subscription, you can access all payroll-related tasks in this section. This includes adding new employees, setting up employee deductions, running payrolls, and making payroll tax payments.
- **Other**: The other section includes making bank deposits, bank transfers, recording journal entries, generating customer statements, and making inventory adjustments.

In this section, we have learned how to access the menus of QBO, all of which give you access to your company information, lists, tools, and profile. In addition, the Quick Create menu allows you to access customers, vendors, employees, and other areas of QuickBooks. Now that you know how to locate information and navigate QBO, we will show you how to customize QuickBooks for your business by setting up your company preferences.

Setting up company preferences in QuickBooks Online

Before you start entering data into QuickBooks, you should spend some time going through company preferences, which allow you to turn on features that you would like to use and deactivate features that you don't plan on using. Click on the gear icon and select account and settings (the following list is the **Your Company** column) to navigate to company preferences.

Company preferences is made up of seven key areas:

- Company
- Billing and subscription
- Usage
- Sales
- Expenses
- Payments
- Advanced

Let's look at each one of these in more detail.

Company

In company preferences, you will provide basic information about your business, such as the contact email and telephone number, where customers can reach you and your mailing address. The contact information that's included in this section will appear on customer invoices and emails that are sent to them so that they know how to get in contact with you. You will also provide your company name and entity type (sole proprietor, partnership, LLC, C-Corp, or S-Corp). A brief explanation of these entity types is as follows:

- **Sole proprietor**: A business that has one owner. Sole proprietors generally file a Schedule C to report their business income and expenses, along with IRS Form 1040.
- **Partnership**: A business with two or more owners. Partnerships generally file IRS Form 1065 to report their business income and expenses to the Internal Revenue Service.
- **Limited Liability Company** (**LLC**): A company with one or more owners who are not personally liable for the LLC's debts or lawsuits.

- **C-Corp**: A corporation that is taxed separately from its owners. Corporations typically file IRS Form 1020 to report business income and expenses.
- **S-Corp**: A closely held corporation that elects to be taxed under IRS Subchapter S. S-Corps typically file IRS Form 1020S to report business income and expenses.

Once you have filled in the **Company** settings, this page should resemble the one for our fictitious company, Photos By Design, LLC, as shown in the following screenshot:

Company name		
	Company name	Photos By Design, LLC
	Legal name	*Same as company name*
	EIN	12-3456789
Company type	Tax form	Limited liability
	Industry	Photography Studios, Portrait
Contact info	Company email	info@photosbydesign.com
	Customer-facing email	*Same as company email*
	Company phone	310-555-1234
	Website	www.photosbydesign
Address	Company address	1234 Beverly Drive, Beverly Hills, CA 90210
	Customer-facing address	*Same as company address*
	Legal address	*Same as company address*

The information you provide in company preferences can impact several areas of QuickBooks, such as customer invoices, tax forms, and documents. Therefore, it's important to complete this information in its entirety before you begin using QuickBooks to track your business activity. Next, we will explain what information you will find in the billing and subscription section.

Billing and subscription

The billing and subscription settings allow you to provide details of the QuickBooks Online plan you have subscribed to.

Once you have completed the **Billing and Subscription** settings, it should resemble the one for our fictitious company, Photos By Design, LLC, as shown in the following screenshot:

Company ID: ▒▒▒ ▒▒▒ ▒▒▒ ▒▒		
QuickBooks ❶	Subscription status	Trial ends in 30 days! Subscribe Now
	Plan details	**QuickBooks Plus** Upgrade ⬆ | Downgrade Free until 06/11/2019 **$70.00/month + applicable taxes**
	Next Charge	**Free through 06/11/2019**
Payroll ❷	Subscription status	**Not subscribed** Learn More
Payments ❸	Subscription status	**Not subscribed** Apply now | Connect an existing QuickBooks Payments account Let your customers pay you online, instantly from invoices
Checks ❹	Checks and supplies	Order checks & supplies | Order 1099s & W2s

A brief description of the information you will find in the billing and subscription settings is as follows:

1. **QuickBooks**: Your subscription status will appear in this section. If you are currently using a trial version, it will show you the date the trial expires. You can click the upgrade or downgrade buttons if you would like to change your subscription plan.

2. **Payroll**: If you have subscribed to payroll, the details of your payroll plan will be in this section. If you would like to subscribe to a payroll, click on the **Learn More** link and follow the on-screen prompts to review and select a payroll plan.

3. **Payments:** If you would like to accept online payments from customers, sign up for Intuit Payments services. With this service, your customers can pay their invoices online via ACH bank transfer, debit card, or credit card. Click on the **Apply Now** link to sign up, but note that additional fees will apply.

4. **Checks**: If you write a lot of checks to pay bills, you should consider printing checks directly from QuickBooks. You can order checks from Intuit by clicking on the **Order checks & supplies** link in this section. You can also order checks through your bank.

Now that you know how to review your subscription status and what services you are subscribed to, you need to know what your usage limits are. We will discuss what usage limits are and how they can affect your QBO subscription next.

Usage

In April 2019, Intuit implemented usage limits on all QuickBooks Online plans. What this means is that each plan will have a maximum number of billable users, classes, locations, and charts of accounts. The following is a brief description of these:

- **Billable users**: The total number of users you can give access to your QuickBooks Online account. This would include a bookkeeper, accountant, or employees.
- **Classes**: Depending on your business, a class can represent departments, office locations, or product lines. Each plan now has a cap on the number of classes that can be created.

- **Locations**: If you have multiple locations, you can turn on location tracking in QuickBooks. Each plan now has a cap on the number of locations that can be created.
- **Chart of accounts**: We discussed the chart of accounts in the *Bookkeeping basics* section of `Chapter 1`, *Getting Started with QuickBooks Online*. The chart of accounts is used to classify your day-to-day business transactions. For example, office supplies and telephone expenses are two accounts that appear on the chart of accounts. Each QBO plan now has a cap on the number of accounts you can add to the chart of accounts list.

The following is a summary table that includes the usage limits for each QuickBooks Online plan:

	QBO Simple Start	QBO Essentials	QBO Plus	QBO Advanced
Classes and locations (combined)	0	0	40	Unlimited
Chart of accounts	250	250	250	Unlimited
Billable users	1	3	5	25

The following is a brief explanation of the usage limits for each QuickBooks Online plan:

- **QuickBooks Simple Start:** QBO Simple Start does not have the ability to track classes or locations. You can have up to 250 accounts on the chart of accounts list. You can have one billable user and two accountant users with this plan.
- **QuickBooks Online Essentials:** Similar to Simple Start, QBO Essentials does not have the ability to track classes or locations. You can have up to 250 accounts on the chart of accounts list. Three billable users (that is, bookkeepers or employees) and two accountant users are included with this plan.
- **QuickBooks Online Plus:** QBO Plus allows you to track classes and locations. You can add up to a total of 40 classes and/or locations. Five billable users and two accountant users are included with this plan.
- **QuickBooks Online Advanced:** QBO Advanced allows you to track classes and locations. You can add unlimited classes and/or locations. In addition, 25 billable users and two accountant users are included with this plan.

Your usage settings should resemble the ones for our fictitious company, Photos By Design, LLC, as shown in the following screenshot:

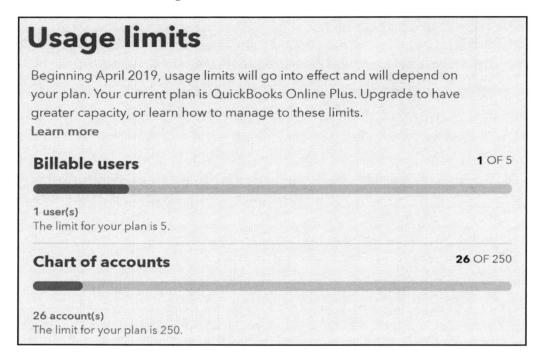

As we mentioned previously, usage limits can impact the number of users you can add to QBO and the classes, locations, and accounts you add to the chart of accounts. This can have a significant effect on how much you pay for your QBO subscription if you hit the maximum usage settings and need to upgrade.

Sales

The Sales settings allow you to select and customize an invoice, estimates, and sales receipt templates. In this section, you will set payment terms for customers. If you have a few customers whose payment terms differ, you can customize payment terms when you add a new customer. If you offer discounts to customers or require upfront deposits, you can turn on these features here.

The following is a screenshot of the settings for Sales:

Customize ①	Customize the way forms look to your customers	Customize look and feel
Sales form content ②	Preferred invoice terms	Net 30
	Preferred delivery method	None
	Shipping	Off
	Custom fields	Off
	Custom transaction numbers	Off
	Service date	Off
	Discount	Off
	Deposit	Off
	Tips (Gratuity)	Off
Products and services ③	Show Product/Service column on sales forms	On
	Show SKU column	Off
	Turn on price rules BETA	Off
	Track quantity and price/rate	On
	Track inventory quantity on hand	Off
④ **Progress Invoicing**	Create multiple partial invoices from a single estimate	On
Messages ⑤	Default email message sent with sales forms	
Reminders ⑥	Default email message sent with reminders	
Online delivery ⑦	Email options for all sales forms	
Statements ⑧	Show aging table at bottom of statement	On

The following is a brief explanation of the information you can update/change in the Sales settings:

1. **Customize:** This setting allows you to customize the look and feel of the invoices, estimates, and sales receipt forms. By clicking on the **customize look and feel** button, you will be able to select a template design, add your company logo, colors, and font, and determine what information you would like to appear on each form.

2. **Sales form content**: In this section, you can select the default payment terms for most customers. For example, if the invoice due date for most customers is Net 30 days, you will make that selection in the preferred invoice terms field (shown in the preceding screenshot). If you have customers that have different payment terms, you can select those when you add the customer to QuickBooks. If you offer discounts, accept deposits, or want to add custom fields, you will also turn these features on in this section.

3. **Products and services**: The products and services settings allow you to determine what information you would like to appear on the sales form. You can turn on price rules, which is a feature that allows you to set up automatic discounts for certain customers or on specific products and services. If you want to track inventory, you will need to turn on both the **Track quantity and price/rate** and the **Track inventory quantity on hand** features.

4. **Progress invoicing**: Progress invoicing allows you to bill a customer in installments. For example, let's say you have a job that is going to result in $100,000 in revenue but you are required to complete certain milestones before you can submit an invoice. Progress billing allows you to create multiple invoices for one job. QuickBooks allows you to run reports that will show you how much you have billed against the job and the remaining amount to be billed.

5. **Messages**: When you email invoices, sales receipts, or estimates directly from QuickBooks, you can customize the message that is included in the body of the email. You can also select whether you want the invoice to be attached to the email as a PDF document or if you prefer the invoice details to be included in the body of the email.

6. **Reminders**: QuickBooks allows you to send payment reminder emails to customers. You can customize the message that goes out to your customers in this section.

7. **Online delivery**: Online delivery allows you to select the format of all the sales forms that will go out to customers. The options are PDF, HTML, or a link to the online invoice. The selections that are made here will affect all invoices, sales receipts, and estimates that are emailed directly from QuickBooks.

8. **Statements**: If you prefer to send statements to customers, you can select from two types of formats. You can have each transaction listed as a single line on the statement or you can list each transaction and the details on the statement.

Now that you know how to customize sales forms, set payment terms for customers, and turn on discounts and deposits, it's time to learn how to manage expenses. We will discuss Expense settings next.

Expenses

The settings in the Expenses section are centered around preferences for managing bills, expenses, and purchase orders. In this section, you will determine what information you want to appear on expense and purchase forms, whether or not you want to track expenses and items by customer, and select default payment terms.

The following is a screenshot of the Expense settings:

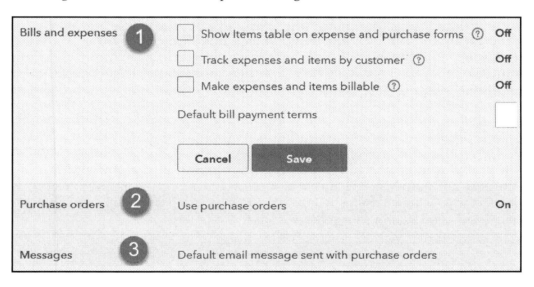

The following is a brief explanation of what you can find in the Expense settings:

1. **Bills and expenses**: This section includes the following three options for tracking expenses:

   - **Show items table on expense and purchase forms**: Selecting this box will add a *products and services* table to your expense and purchase forms so that you can itemize your products and services.
   - **Track expenses and items by customer**: This feature allows you to tag expenses with a specific customer. This is ideal for reporting purposes if you want to keep track of specific items that have been purchased but aren't billable to customers.
   - **Make expenses and items billable**: This feature adds a billable column on all expense and purchase forms so that you can bill customers for items you've purchased on their behalf.

2. **Purchase orders**: If you plan to create purchase orders, be sure to turn this feature on. However, if you don't need to create purchase orders, you can leave it turned off.

3. **Messages**: You can email purchase orders directly from QuickBooks to vendor suppliers. This section allows you to customize the email message that your vendor supplier will receive along with the purchase orders.

Now that you are familiar with the expense settings that affect bills, purchase orders, and expenses, you can set up QuickBooks the way you need to in order to track expenses that are incurred by your business. Next, we will discuss a way for you to get paid faster by your customers by using QuickBooks Payments.

Payments

QuickBooks Payments allows you to accept online payments from customers in the form of wire transfers, debit cards, and credit cards. Once approved, all the invoices that you email to customers will include a payment link. Your customers can click on the link, enter their payment details, and submit a payment in just a few minutes.

To apply for a **QuickBooks Payments** account, click on the **Learn more** button, as shown in the following screenshot:

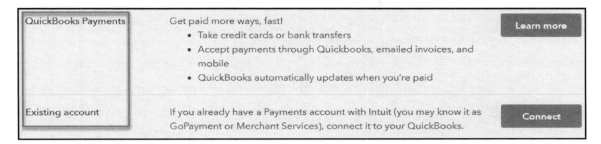

If you have an existing payments account, you can connect it by clicking the **Connect** button and following the on-screen instructions.

As we mentioned previously, QuickBooks Payments makes it easier to get paid by customers in a timely manner. Customers can quickly pay their invoices online with a debit card, credit card, or wire transfer. This will allow you to maintain a positive cash flow, which is important for your business.

Advanced

The Advanced settings page includes nine main settings: accounting, company type, chart of accounts, categories, automation, projects, time tracking, currency, and other preferences.

The following is a screenshot of the **Advanced settings** section:

Accounting ①	First month of fiscal year	January
	First month of income tax year	Same as fiscal year
	Accounting method	Accrual
	Close the books	Off
Company type ②	Tax form	Limited liability
Chart of accounts ③	Enable account numbers	Off
	Tips account	
Categories ④	Track classes	Off
	Track locations	Off
Automation ⑤	Pre-fill forms with previously entered content	On
	Automatically apply credits	On
	Automatically invoice unbilled activity	Off
	Automatically apply bill payments	On
Projects ⑥	Organize all job-related activity in one place	On
Time tracking ⑦	Add Service field to timesheets	Off
	Make Single-Time Activity Billable to Customer	On
Currency ⑧	Home Currency	United States Dollar
	Multicurrency	Off
Other preferences ⑨	Date format	MM/dd/yyyy
	Number format	123,456.00
	Customer label	Customers
	Warn if duplicate check number is used	On
	Warn if duplicate bill number is used	Off
	Sign me out if inactive for	1 hour

A brief description of what information is included in the Advanced settings section is as follows:

1. **Accounting**: In the accounting settings, you will select the first month of your fiscal year and income tax year, which may be the same. You will indicate your accounting method (for example, cash or accrual) and there is an option to close the books. **Close the books** allows you to prevent any changes being made to your financial data after a certain date. For example, once you have filed your tax returns for the year, you should enter the last day of the previous year as your closing date (for example, 12/31/2018). This will ensure that information dated 12/31/2018 and prior cannot be changed.

2. **Company type**: In this field, you will select the structure of your business. The common business structures are sole proprietor, partnership, limited liability, C-corporation, and S-Corporation.

3. **Chart of accounts**: As we discussed in `Chapter 1`, *Getting Started with QuickBooks Online*, the chart of accounts is a way to categorize your day-to-day business transactions. You have the option to assign account numbers to your chart of accounts list by turning on the **Enable account numbers** preference.

4. **Categories**: There are two types of categories in QuickBooks: classes and locations. **Classes** are generally used to track income and expenses for departments or product lines. **Locations** are used to track income and expenses for multiple locations of your business. These preferences must be turned on in order for you to use them.

5. **Automation**: You can save time by automating certain tasks. QuickBooks will automatically prefill forms based on the information you have provided in a previous transaction for a customer or vendor. You can also allow QuickBooks to automatically apply credit that's been received from vendor suppliers and bill payments.

6. **Projects**: The projects feature allows you to keep track of all income and expenses for jobs/projects that you are working on.

7. **Time tracking**: If you need to track hours for employees, contractors, or yourself, you can easily do this in QuickBooks. You can also bill customers for hours you've worked by transferring the hours to customer invoices.

8. **Currency**: QuickBooks allows you to create invoices and pay bills in multiple currencies. You can do business with vendor suppliers and customers across the globe by providing invoices in their native currency. All of your financial reports can be generated in your home currency or any currency that you choose.

Once you turn on the multicurrency feature, it cannot be turned off. This is because there are several conversion tables that are activated in the background once you turn this feature on and start using it.

9. **Other preferences**: The other preferences section involves general formatting preferences for the date and numbers that appear throughout the program. You can also select the type of label for your customers. For example, if you are a nonprofit organization, you can select **donors**, and if you are a real estate investor, you can select **tenants**. This nomenclature will appear throughout the program. This preference also includes a warning if you use a duplicate check number or vendor invoice number. You should turn both of these features on to help you avoid duplicate payments. For security reasons, QBO will automatically sign you out after you have been inactive for 1 hour. However, you can change this setting to a maximum of 3 hours.

You now know that accounting settings affect several areas of QuickBooks. You can determine your chart of accounts structure, turn on time tracking, set your home currency, and turn on the multi-currency feature if you do business in other countries. In addition, you can turn on the projects and categories features for additional tracking of income and expenses.

Summary

In this chapter, we have covered setting up our QuickBooks Online account and basic navigation using dashboards, icons, and online menus in QuickBooks Online. We have also shown you how to customize the company settings, which includes billing and subscription, usage limits, sales, expenses, payments, and advanced options. Taking the time to set up your company file will help you save time in the long run because you won't have to do it later on. Plus, you won't have to worry about customer invoices or vendor bills missing key information because your company file wasn't set up properly.

In the next chapter, we will pick up where this one left off by continuing to customize QuickBooks for our business. We will also cover customizing the chart of accounts, show you how to connect your bank and credit card accounts to QuickBooks, and walk you through giving other users access to your QuickBooks data.

Migrating to QuickBooks Online 3

Whether you are currently using another form of accounting software or spreadsheets to manage the books for your business, you will need to gather a few key documents and information to migrate over to **QuickBooks Online (QBO)**. In addition, the date on which you decide to implement QuickBooks will also determine what information is required for a smooth migration. Providing all of the information required will ensure that QuickBooks is properly set up prior to you using it to track your business income and expenses. Otherwise, you could encounter inaccurate and unreliable financial statements, which will make it difficult to know your business' overall health and make filing taxes difficult.

In this chapter, we will show you how to convert from another form of accounting software or Excel to QuickBooks Online. If you are currently using **QuickBooks Desktop (QBD)**, we will show you how to convert from QBD to QuickBooks Online.

In this chapter, we will cover the following six key concepts:

- Key information and documents required to convert to QuickBooks Online
- Questions to ask yourself in preparation for data conversion
- Choosing your QuickBooks start date
- Converting from another accounting software or Excel to QuickBooks Online
- Converting from QuickBooks Desktop to QuickBooks Online
- Converting from QuickBooks Desktop data to QuickBooks Online

Key information and documents required to convert to QuickBooks Online

Before we get into the mechanics of converting data to QuickBooks Online, you will need to gather some key documents and answer a few questions first. This information is necessary so that we can customize QuickBooks for your business. Plus, having this information at your fingertips will help you to complete the company setup a lot faster.

The information you will need to know includes the following:

- **Company name**: This needs to be the legal name of the business.
- **Company contact information**: This will include the mailing address, business telephone number, business email address, and website address of the company.
- **Industry**: In QuickBooks, you will select the industry that your business falls into. Using this information, a default chart of accounts list will be created for you.
- **Federal tax ID number**: A nine-digit number that identifies your business to the IRS. If you don't have a federal tax ID number, you can use your social security number.
- **Company organization type**: In QuickBooks, you will need to select from one of the following organization types: sole proprietor, LLC, nonprofit, C-corporation, or S-corporation.
- **Fiscal year**: In QuickBooks, you will need to enter your company fiscal year. For example, if you are on a calendar year, it will be January 1 to December 31.
- **List of products you sell**: If you have a lot of products and services, you should create an Excel or CSV spreadsheet that includes the product name, product description, cost, price, and quantity on-hand. This information can be imported into QuickBooks in just a few minutes.
- **List of services you sell**: Similar to products, you should create an Excel or CSV spreadsheet that includes the name of the service, a brief description, and the price. You can import this information into QuickBooks.
- **List of sales tax rates**: A list of each city, state, or jurisdiction for which you are required to collect sales, along with the name of the tax authority that you pay, is required to properly set up sales tax in QuickBooks.
- **List of customers**: Customer contact details, such as an address, email address, telephone number, Facebook address, or other information you have on file should be entered into an Excel or CSV file so that you can import the information into QuickBooks.
- **List of vendor suppliers**: Vendor contact details, such as remit to address, email address, telephone number, primary contacts, and other information you have on file should be entered into an Excel or CSV file so that you can import it into QuickBooks.
- **Chart of accounts list**: Your current list of accounts should be entered into an Excel spreadsheet so that you can easily import it into QuickBooks.

As discussed, having access to key documents and information about your business will help you to properly set up your company file. This is important to ensure you are not missing key information when you create forms such as customer invoices, as well as to ensure your financial statements are accurate and reliable.

Questions to ask yourself in preparation for data conversion

When setting up your QuickBooks company file, you will need to determine whether you want to bring over any data from your existing accounting program. Additionally, you need to know what features you want to use in QuickBooks. Answering the following questions will help determine what type of setup you need to manage your day-to-day business activities:

- **How much historical data do you want to bring over to QuickBooks?**

  If you are converting in the middle of the year, you need to determine whether you will bring over all of the transactions that have occurred thus far, or just start from the current month you are in. The benefit of bringing over transactions that go back to the beginning of the year is that it will allow you to run financial statements in QuickBooks for the entire year, as opposed to only half of the year. Keep in mind that it will be more time-consuming to do this, so you will need to weigh the cost versus the benefit to determine whether or not it is worth it.

- **How much detailed information do you want to bring over to QuickBooks?**

  If you do decide to bring over the historical information for an entire year, you've got two options. First, you can enter each transaction individually into QuickBooks. Depending on how much data you have, this could be quite labor-intensive and expensive if you have to pay someone else to do it. Second, you can create a summary journal that is a lot faster than entering each individual transaction, but you will not have the details in QuickBooks. If you have a ton of transactions, this is going to be the best option for you. However, if you don't have a lot of activity, then enter transactions individually.

- **Do you create estimates or proposals for existing or prospective customers?**

  You can easily create estimates or proposals for customers in QuickBooks. A couple of benefits to doing this are that you can easily email estimates, and track the status of when the estimate is approved or not approved by customers.

- **Do you plan to create billing statements for customers?**

Depending on the type of business you own, you may want to generate billing statements for customers on a weekly, monthly, or quarterly basis. This is common for doctor's offices and for companies that provide services to customers on a recurring basis (for example, monthly, quarterly, or annually).

- **Do you want to use invoices to bill customers?**

Invoices are commonly used to bill customers to whom you have extended credit terms. This means that payment is not due when you provide goods and/or services. Instead, you send these customers an invoice that includes a due date, and they are expected to remit payment before or by the due date. For example, Net 30 payment terms mean that the bill is due 30 days after the date on the invoice.

- **Do you want to keep track of your bills through QuickBooks?**

If you have a lot of bills to keep track of, you should consider entering all bills into QuickBooks. Once you enter a bill into QuickBooks, it will alert you when the bill is getting close to the due date. You can pay the bill through online banking, or you can pay the bill by writing a check directly from QuickBooks. If you don't receive a lot of paper bills, then it may not be ideal to track unpaid bills through QuickBooks. Instead, you can track bills as they are paid from your bank/credit card account.

- **Do you want to keep track of inventory through QuickBooks?**

If you need to keep track of inventory purchases by tracking quantities and costs, then you need to track the inventory in QuickBooks. However, if you prefer to keep track of sales only, there is no need to turn on the inventory tracking feature in QuickBooks Online.

- **Do you have employees or 1099 contractors?**

If you have employees who you need to track in QuickBooks, see `Chapter 13`, *Managing Payroll in QuickBooks Online*, on how to set up and track payroll in QuickBooks. All 1099 contractors should be set up as vendors in QuickBooks. Make sure you add them to the list of vendors that you will import into QuickBooks.

- **Do you need to track by department or location?**

  If you need to track income and expenses by department or business segment, you will need to turn on class tracking. You can also turn on location tracking if you have more than one store or office location you need to keep track of.

Similar to the key information and documents discussed in the previous section, it's important for you to think about how you want to use QuickBooks. Answering a few simple questions can help you determine what features you need to turn on in QBO to manage your books. Another key component to getting your books set up is choosing your QuickBooks start date. We will discuss this in detail next.

Choosing your QuickBooks start date

One of the most important decisions you will make is what your QuickBooks start date will be. The start date is based on how much historical information you decide to bring over from your existing accounting software into QuickBooks Online. Let's take a look at a few examples:

- **Example 1**: Let's say a web designer decided to start a business in January. The start date in QuickBooks for this brand new business would be January 1.
- **Example 2**: Let's assume it's January 2020 and you have decided to bring in data from January 1 through December 31, 2019. Your QuickBooks start date will be December 31, 2019. That way, all 2019 balances will be as of this date, and transactions dated January 1, 2020, and after will be directly entered into QuickBooks Online.
- **Example 3**: Let's take our web designer from the first example, but this time, we don't want to bring over any historical data. Instead, we just want to start using QuickBooks in January 2020. The start date would be January 1, 2020, since no historical data will be converted over to QuickBooks.

After reviewing the examples, you should have an idea of how to determine your QuickBooks start date. As discussed, this is a critical decision when it comes to deciding how much historical data to bring over from your existing accounting software. If you are converting from another accounting software or Excel, we will discuss in detail how to convert your data over to QuickBooks Online next.

Converting from another accounting software or Excel to QuickBooks Online

There are four primary steps for converting from another accounting software or Excel spreadsheet into QuickBooks Online:

1. Complete the initial company file setup.
2. Import all of your list information for customers, vendors, and products and services.
3. Import your chart of accounts list, or update the default listing in QuickBooks to match your current list.
4. Verify the accuracy of the data that has been converted.

In Chapter 2, *Company File Setup*, we covered in detail how to complete the initial company file setup.

In this chapter, we will cover the other two options you have for entering data into QuickBooks: recording details of historical data, and recording a summary journal entry of historical data. We will look at the correct order in which to enter historical transactions, and how to verify the accuracy of the data.

Recording details of historical data in QuickBooks Online

As mentioned previously, the ideal method of entering historical data into QuickBooks Online is to enter individual transactions. While this is more time-consuming than completing a summary journal entry, it includes all of the details of each transaction.

Individual transactions must be entered in the correct order to avoid any issues. The order in which to enter historical transactions into QuickBooks Online is as follows:

1. Purchase orders; bills and payments; credits from vendors; credit card charges; checks; inventory on hand
2. Employee timesheets, billable hours
3. Invoices, sales receipts, credit memos, returns
4. Customer payments, bank deposits

5. Sales taxes paid, payroll transactions
6. All banking transactions (not previously entered); credit card transactions (not previously entered); reconcile all bank and credit card accounts

Now that you know the correct order to enter historical data, it's important that you follow these steps to avoid issues later on. If you don't have the time to enter individual transactions, you can opt for recording a summary journal entry. We will discuss how to do this next.

Recording a summary journal entry of historical data in QuickBooks Online

A summary journal entry will only include lump sum total amounts. To enter balances for balance sheet accounts, you should run a balance sheet report in your current accounting system for the last day of the year for which you are bringing over data. If you would like to also bring over income and expense data, you need to print an income statement from your existing accounting system, as of the last day of the year for which you are bringing over data. Enter the totals for each account into QuickBooks.

Make sure the accounts that appear on both the balance sheet and income statement reports have been created in QuickBooks before you create the journal entry.

Follow these steps to create a journal entry in QuickBooks Online:

1. Navigate to the **Journal Entry** screen by clicking on the plus (+) sign in the upper right-hand corner of the home page, as indicated here:

2. Right below the **Other** column, click on **Journal Entry**, as follows:

3. Complete the fields in the **Journal Entry** form:

To complete the **Journal Entry** form, you will need to complete eight fields. Here is a brief explanation of what information to include in each field (shown in the preceding screenshot):

1. **Journal date**: Enter the effective date of the journal entry. For example, you would enter the last date of the fiscal year for which you are bringing data over (for example, December 31, 20XX).

2. **Journal no**: QuickBooks will automatically assign a journal entry number, beginning with **1**. However, you can start with a different number, such as **1000**, and QuickBooks will automatically increment each journal number thereafter.

3. **Is Adjusting Journal Entry?**: In general, if you are recording journals in order to close the books, those journals are generally considered adjusting journal entries and should be marked as such. Otherwise, most journal entries will not need to be flagged as adjusting.

4. **ACCOUNT**: From the drop-down menu, select the account(s) that require debeting. After all debits have been entered, you can enter the accounts that will be credited right after.

5. **DEBITS**: Enter the debit amount in this field.

6. **CREDITS**: Enter the credit amount in this field.

7. **DESCRIPTION**: Enter a brief description of the purpose of the journal entry (for example, to bring over existing balances as of December 31, 2019).

8. **NAME**: If a line item is for a specific customer, you can select the appropriate customer from the drop-down menu.

The **NAME** field is used in those instances when you are making an adjustment to the accounts receivable balance for a specific customer.

Now that you know the two methods used to enter historical data into QBO, you can decide which method will work best for you. If you are a current QuickBooks Desktop user, there is some additional information you need to know. We will cover converting from QuickBooks Desktop to QuickBooks Online next.

Converting from QuickBooks Desktop to QuickBooks Online

If you are in the process of deciding whether to convert from QuickBooks Desktop to QuickBooks Online, you need to review the list of key features that you may currently use in QuickBooks Desktop but that are not available in QuickBooks Online. Additionally, you need to review the list of data that will not convert from QuickBooks Desktop to QuickBooks Online. This is important because there may be features not available in QBO that you need to run your business. You also need to determine whether you can do without the information that does not convert over to QBO. We will explore these ideas in the next two sections.

Functionality not available in QuickBooks Online

QuickBooks Online does not include the ability to create sales orders, manage fixed assets, create price levels, or generate an estimate to actual reporting. Therefore, I do not recommend you convert from QuickBooks Desktop to QuickBooks Online if you need the following features:

- **Sales orders:** A form used to record and track customer orders. A sales order will commit the quantity ordered or trigger a backorder if the product is out of stock.
- **Fixed asset tracking with Fixed Asset Manager**: Fixed asset tracking includes keeping track of the cost of fixed assets purchased, calculating depreciation, and the current value of assets.
- **Price levels**: Price levels allow you to give customers a bulk discount for all items purchased or for specific items purchased.

If you currently use these features in QuickBooks Desktop, you should either find a workaround in QBO or postpone converting over to QBO if they are critical to your business. As discussed, there is certain data that will not convert to QuickBooks Online. We will explain data that will not convert from QuickBooks Desktop to QuickBooks Online next.

QuickBooks Desktop data that will not convert to QuickBooks Online

As we mentioned previously, QuickBooks Desktop and QuickBooks Online are two completely different products. QuickBooks Desktop is available for Windows or iOS platforms, whereas QuickBooks Online is a cloud-based software. With that said, there are several data points that will not convert to QuickBooks Online.

The following table provides a summary of the data that will not convert to QuickBooks Online, along with a workaround in QuickBooks Online:

QuickBooks Desktop data that will not convert to QuickBooks Online	Workaround in QuickBooks Online
Custom sales form templates for estimates, invoices, and sales receipts	Create new templates using the built-in template layout designer
The bank and credit card connections, and the downloaded bank activity pending review	Re-establish connection in QBO for all bank and credit card accounts. Review all transactions prior to proceeding with the conversion.

QuickBooks users and permissions	Create each user with the appropriate permissions
Reconciliation reports for all bank and credit card accounts previously reconciled	Since the reconciled status **R** will convert, do one big reconciliation, or redo them individually to recreate the reports
Memorized reports	Re-create reports that you run often, and save them in Favorites
Audit trail report with historical activity	Print and save the audit trail report. Refer to the backup QuickBooks file.
The connection to your QuickBooks payments merchant services account	Connect your QuickBooks payments merchant services account to QuickBooks Online
Balance sheet budgets	QuickBooks Online Plus does not allow you to create balance sheet budgets. However, you can create profit and loss budgets.
Closing date password and accumulated closing date exceptions	QBO will track new exceptions from the date of the conversion

Now that you are familiar with the data that will not convert from QuickBooks Desktop to QuickBooks Online, you can determine whether the workaround is an ideal solution, or if you can run your business without bringing over certain data. After having compiled key information, asked yourself a few questions, chosen your start date, and familiarized yourself with the data that will not convert, you are ready to convert your data. We will discuss converting from QuickBooks Desktop data to QuickBooks Online next.

Converting from QuickBooks Desktop data to QuickBooks Online

Now that you are familiar with most of the limitations of converting data from QuickBooks Desktop to QuickBooks Online, we will walk through the steps on how to convert your data from QBD to QBO. There are seven primary steps involved with converting data from QuickBooks Desktop to Online:

- Checking the target count
- Creating a QuickBooks Online account
- Backing up your QuickBooks Desktop file
- Checking for updates

- Running the QuickBooks Desktop conversion to the QuickBooks Online tool
- Logging in to QuickBooks Online
- Verifying that all of your data was converted

Let's take a look at each of these steps, one by one.

Checking the target count

The current data limit is 350K, in targets to import historical transactions. In order to convert your Desktop data to Online, your data limit must not exceed 350K. To check your target count, open your QuickBooks file. From the home page, press *F2*, which will open the **Product Information** screen. You will find your product license number, the location of your company file, and other key data points, such as the target count.

The following screenshot includes an example of the target count on the **Product Information** screen. For this company file, the target count is 3,731, which is well below the 350K limit:

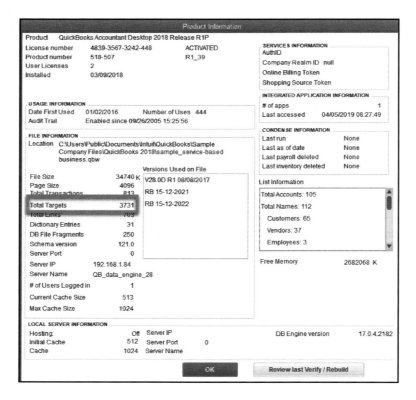

After verifying that your QuickBooks file is below the 350K limit, you can proceed to create a QuickBooks Online account. In the next section, we will show you how to create your QuickBooks Online account for your business.

Creating a QuickBooks Online account

Prior to converting your data, you must already have a QBO account.

Follow these steps to create a QuickBooks Online account:

1. Go to www.intuit.com.
2. Click on **Plans & Pricing**.
3. Choose one of the following versions of QuickBooks Online:

    - **Simple Start**
    - **Essentials**
    - **Plus**
    - **Advanced**

4. Enter your company information.
5. Log out of your account.

After creating your QuickBooks Online account, you are ready to convert your data. Before converting your Desktop data, it's important to save a backup of your QuickBooks file. If there is an error with converting your data, you can always refer back to the backup file if you need to. Let's walk through backing up your QuickBooks Desktop file.

Backing up your QuickBooks Desktop file

Converting your data does not change it. However, you should always have a backup copy of your data prior to conversion.

Follow these steps to create a backup copy of your QuickBooks file:

1. Click on the **File** menu.
2. Select **Create Copy.**
3. Select **Backup copy**, as indicated in the following screenshot:

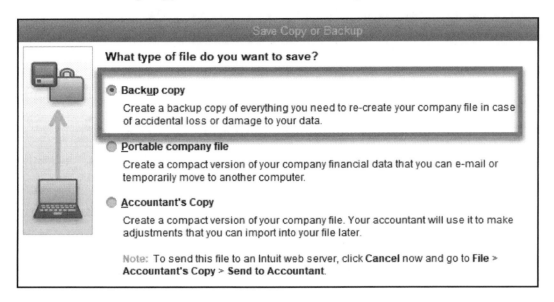

Now that you have a backup copy of your QuickBooks Desktop data, you can proceed with the conversion. To avoid errors when converting your data, you need to ensure that you are working with the latest version of QuickBooks Desktop. Next, we will show you how to check for updates to your software.

Checking for updates

Before using the conversion tool, you need to make sure you have the most recent conversion tool. For QuickBooks Pro, Premier, and Enterprise users, follow these instructions to check for updates:

1. From the **Help** menu at the very top of the home page, select **Update QuickBooks Desktop**, as indicated here:

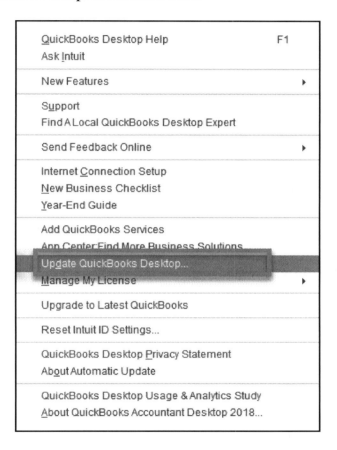

2. Next, click on the **Update Now** tab, select **All Updates** by putting a checkmark in the first column to select the available updates, and select **Get Updates**, as indicated in the following screenshot:

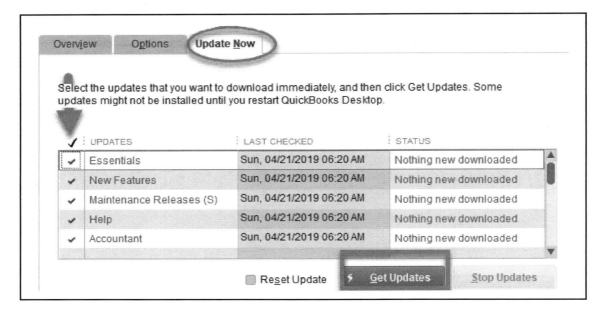

Now that your QuickBooks software has been updated to the most recent version, you are ready to run the QuickBooks Desktop conversion to the QBO tool. We will cover this in detail next.

Running the QuickBooks Desktop conversion to the QuickBooks Online tool

There is a QuickBooks Desktop conversion tool within QuickBooks Desktop.

From the **Company** menu, select **Export Company File to QuickBooks Online**, as indicated in the following screenshot:

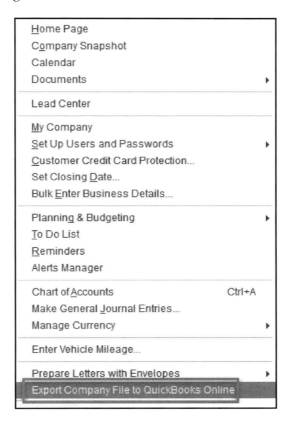

After selecting **Export Company File to QuickBooks Online**, the next screen will allow you to log in to your QBO account that you set up in the *Creating a QuickBooks Online account* section. To complete the QuickBooks Desktop data conversion, log in to your QBO account.

Logging in to QuickBooks Online

After exporting your QuickBooks data file, the login screen for QBO will appear. Follow the steps outlined here:

1. Enter your secure **Email or user ID** and **Password** for your QuickBooks Online account:

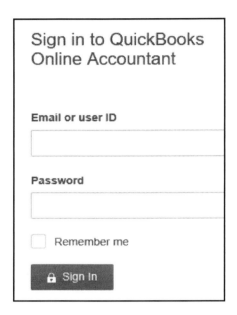

2. Follow the onscreen instructions to complete the upload. The length of time this will take will depend on how large your company file is. Once the upload is complete, you will see an onscreen notification that your data has successfully uploaded. When your data is ready, you will receive an email from the Intuit support team. This generally takes place within 1 to 24 hours, at the most.

After completing all of the steps to export your QuickBooks data file to QBO and you have received an email from the Intuit support team confirming your data has been uploaded, the final step in converting your data is to verify that the data in your QBO file is correct. We will discuss how to do this next.

Verifying that all of your data was converted

The final step in the conversion process is to verify that all of your data was successfully imported into QuickBooks Online. To do this, you need to run a profit and loss report and a balance sheet report in both QuickBooks Online and Desktop. For instructions on how to run these reports in QuickBooks, head over to `Chapter 10`, *Business Overview Reports*. Be sure to use the following report parameters:

- All dates
- Accrual accounting method

Compare the reports to see if they match. If they don't, contact the Intuit support team by clicking on the **Help** menu in your QBO file and then selecting the option to chat with a support rep, or contact them by telephone. A support rep will assist you with troubleshooting any out-of-balance issues.

Once you have verified that your data was successfully converted to QuickBooks Online, you are ready to start using QuickBooks Online to manage your bookkeeping. You should keep the backup file created in the previous section, in case you discover an issue later on.

Summary

We have covered the key concepts you need to know when converting your QuickBooks Desktop data to QuickBooks Online. You now know what key documents and information you need, what questions to ask yourself, how to choose your start date in QuickBooks, how to convert historical data in detail and summary, and the detailed steps to convert your QuickBooks Desktop data to QBO. Once all of your data has been converted and verified, you are ready for the next step.

In the next chapter, we will show you how to customize QuickBooks Online for your business.

4
Customizing QuickBooks for Your Business

Whether you created your QuickBooks Online account from scratch or you transferred your details from another accounting software program, there are some additional areas that you need to set up to further customize QuickBooks Online for your business. In this chapter, we will show you how to add, edit, and delete accounts to customize the chart of accounts for your business. We will walk through the process of connecting your bank and credit card accounts to QBO so that transactions will automatically download. By connecting your bank accounts to QuickBooks, you will reduce, if not eliminate, the need to manually enter these transactions into QuickBooks. If you need to give other users access to your QuickBooks data, you can easily do so. We will show you how to give your bookkeeper, accountant, and other users access to your QuickBooks data.

The following are the key topics that will be covered in this chapter:

- Customizing the chart of accounts
- Connecting bank accounts to QuickBooks Online
- Connecting credit card accounts to QuickBooks Online
- Giving other users access to your QuickBooks data

Customizing the chart of accounts

As we saw in Chapter 1, *Getting Started with QuickBooks Online*, the chart of accounts is a list of accounts that is used to categorize your day-to-day business transactions. It is the backbone of every accounting system, and if it is not set up properly, it can result in inaccurate financial statements. One of the benefits of using QuickBooks is that you don't have to create the chart of accounts from scratch. Based on the industry that you selected when you created your QBO account, QuickBooks will include a preset chart of accounts list. You can customize the chart of accounts by adding, editing, or deleting accounts to fit your business needs. In this section, we will show you how to add, edit, and delete accounts on the chart of accounts list.

How to add a new account to the chart of accounts list

The default chart of accounts list will include a generic list of accounts used by most businesses, with a few custom accounts related to your industry. However, you will most likely need to customize the list based on your accountant's preferences or your own. For example, if you sell products and services, you may want to create an income account for each, as opposed to lumping sales for both into one account.

Go through the following three steps to add a new account to the chart of accounts list:

1. Click on the **Accounting** tab located on the left menu bar and select **Chart of Accounts**, as shown in the following screenshot:

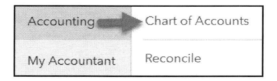

2. Click on the **New** button located in the upper right-hand corner of the screen, directly to the right of the **Run Report** button, as shown in the following screenshot:

3. To create a new account, you will need to provide the account type, the detail account type, the name of the account, and a description of the account, as shown in the following screenshot:

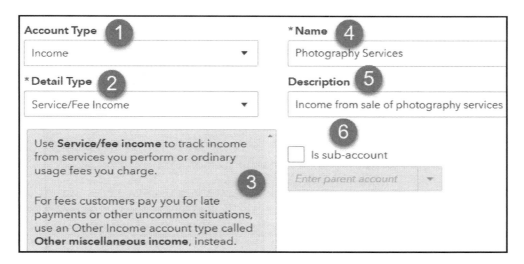

The following list is a brief description of what information should be included in the fields that are labeled in the preceding screenshot:

- **Account Type (1)**: From the drop-down menu, select the account type that the new account should be categorized as. As we saw in `Chapter 1`, *Getting Started with QuickBooks Online*, the five main account types are income, expense, asset, liability, and equity. You will also find other account types in this list, such as fixed assets, bank, and credit card, and they should be used when appropriate.
- **Detail Type (2)**: From the drop-down menu, select the detail type that most accurately describes the type of account you are setting up. The options in the drop-down menu will differ based on the account type selected.
- **Description of detail type (3)**: In this box, QuickBooks will provide you with a detailed explanation of the detail type that you have selected. This should help guide you as to which detail type you should select.
- **Name (4)**: This field will automatically be populated with the detail type you selected. However, you can (and should) change it to something more descriptive, as we have done in the preceding example.
- **Description (5)**: This field is self-explanatory, and should include a brief description of the types of transaction that should be posted to this account.

While you may be tempted to leave the description field blank, I recommend that you don't. It can be useful to include a detailed description so that a bookkeeper or someone who you have hired to manage your books will know what type of transactions belong in this account. If you don't think a description is needed, copy and paste the account name in this field. That way this field will not appear blank on reports.

- **Is sub-account** (6): Sub-accounts are used to provide a more detailed breakdown of an account that is used for multiple types of transactions. For example, it is a good idea to create a main account for car expenses and a sub-account for repairs, registration, and gasoline. Having a detailed break-down of each type of expense will allow you to easily run a report to see how much you have spent on each account.

Once you have completed all of the fields for the new account and saved it, the new account will appear on your chart of accounts list, as shown in the following screenshot:

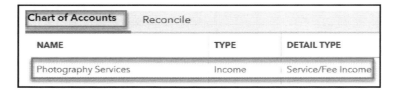

Now that you know how to manually add a new account to the chart of accounts list, you will have a good idea of how long it takes to add a new account. If you need to add more than five accounts, you may want to consider importing new accounts instead of manually entering them. In the next section, we will show you how to import a chart of accounts list from an Excel file.

How to import a chart of accounts list

If your accountant has given you a chart of accounts list that they prefer you to use, you can import that list into QBO. Go through the following steps to import a chart of accounts list:

1. Format your Excel spreadsheet to include the following columns and save it in .csv format:

Account Number	Account Name	Type	Detail Type
112720	Checking Account - Bank of America	Bank	Checking
112721	Money Market - First National Bank	Bank	Money Market
410790	Product Sales Revenue	Income	Sales of Product Income
500780	Cost of Materials	Cost of Goods Sold	Supplies & Materials

2. Click on the arrow to the right of the New button and select **Import** as shown in the following screenshot:

3. Follow the on-screen prompts to complete the import.

Next, we will show you how to edit the chart of accounts list.

How to edit accounts on the chart of accounts list

On occasion, you may want to make changes to an existing account on the chart of account list. You can change the account name and description at any time; however, you can only make changes to the account type and detail type if you have not used the account in a transaction. If you have used the account and then realize that you selected the wrong account type, you will not be able to change it.

Instead, you will need to create the account again from scratch with the correct account or detail type. Once the new account has been created, you need to transfer the transactions that were coded to the wrong account to the new account. After transferring all of the recorded transactions to the new account, you can inactivate the old account.

You can edit accounts on the chart of accounts list by going through the following steps:

1. Click on the **Accounting** tab located on the left menu bar and select **Chart of Accounts**, as shown in the following screenshot:

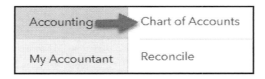

2. Scroll through the chart of accounts list to find the account you want to edit. The following screenshot shows the **Action** column on the far right. Click on the arrow located to the right of **Run report**, as shown in the following screenshot:

NAME ▲	TYPE	DETAIL TYPE	ACTION
Advertising & Marketing	Expenses	Advertising/Promotional	Run report ▼

3. On the next screen, you will see two options: **Edit** and **Make inactive**, as shown in the following screenshot:

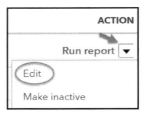

The following is a brief explanation of when you should edit an account and when you should make an account inactive:

- **Edit**: To make changes to the account name, account description, or sub-account, click on the **Edit** button. As we mentioned previously, the only time you can edit the account and detail type is if you have not used the account in any transactions that you have recorded in QuickBooks.
- **Make inactive**: Once you have created an account in QuickBooks, there is no way to delete it. Instead, you will need to inactivate the account. When you inactivate an account in QuickBooks, it will still exist, but it will disappear from the chart of accounts list and will not appear in any drop-down lists. The primary reason for this is that if you have recorded transactions to an account that you decide to stop using, then your transactions will remain in QuickBooks. This is very important in order to maintain accurate financial statements.

4. When you click **Edit**, the current account setup will be displayed. Make the necessary changes, as shown in the following screenshot:

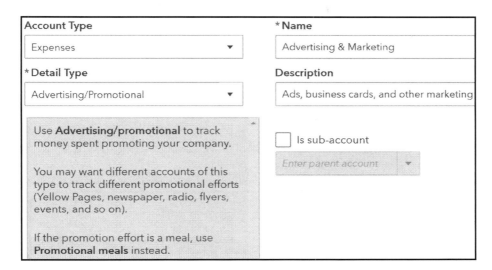

If you have not used the account in a transaction, the account type and detail type fields will also be editable.

In this section, we covered how to make changes to an existing account on your chart of accounts list. We also explained the difference between editing an account and making an account inactive. As previously mentioned, you cannot delete an account, but you can make it inactive. In the next section, we will show you how to inactivate an existing account.

How to inactivate an account on the chart of accounts list

Once you add an account to the chart of accounts, you cannot delete it; however, if you decide that you no longer want to use an account, you can inactivate the account. inactivating an account will remove the account from the chart of the accounts list and the drop-down menus, but it will still exist in the program. This will ensure that any transactions that have been recorded will remain intact, which will also ensure that you have accurate financial statements.

To inactivate an account, go through the following steps:

1. Click on the **Accounting** tab located on the left menu bar and select **Chart of Accounts**, as shown in the following screenshot:

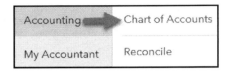

2. Scroll through the chart of accounts list to find the account you want to edit. In the **Action** column on the far right, click on the arrow located to the right of **Run report**, as shown in the following screenshot:

3. Select **Make inactive** from the drop-down arrow, as shown in the following screenshot:

4. You will then receive a message similar to the one shown in the following screenshot, asking you to confirm that you would like to inactivate the account:

5. Click **Yes** to proceed with the inactivation or **No** to leave the account active. If you decide to activate an account that was previously made inactive, you can easily do this by selecting **Make active** to the right of the account from the chart of accounts list, as shown in the following screenshot:

NAME ▲	TYPE	DETAIL TYPE	ACTION
Advertising & Marketing (deleted)	Expenses	Advertising/Promotional	➡ Make active ▼

You now know how to add an account, import a chart of accounts list, edit an account, and inactivate an account on the chart of accounts list. As previously mentioned, the chart of accounts is the backbone of the system. Now that you know how to manage your chart of accounts list, you can be confident that your financial statements will be accurate. In the next section, we will show you how to reduce the number of transactions entered manually by connecting your bank accounts to QuickBooks. In the long run, this will save you a lot of time.

Connecting bank accounts to QuickBooks Online

One of the best features of using cloud accounting software such as QBO is the ability to connect your bank account to the software, so that your books are always up to date with the most recent deposits and withdrawals that have been made to your bank accounts.

There are two ways in which you can update QuickBooks with your banking activity. You can connect your bank account to QuickBooks so that transactions import automatically into QuickBooks, or you can upload transactions from an Excel spreadsheet. We will walk you through each of these processes in more detail now.

Importing banking transactions automatically

There are several benefits to importing your banking transactions automatically. First, you will save a ton of time because you won't have to enter transactions manually. Second, QuickBooks will be updated on a *daily* basis with the most recent banking activity on your account. And finally, it will be a breeze to reconcile your bank account on a daily, weekly, or monthly basis.

Go through the following five steps to import banking transactions automatically into QuickBooks Online:

1. Select **Banking** from the left menu bar, as shown in the following screenshot:

2. On the following screen, you will see a link to a short video tutorial that is a demo of how the banking center works. Click on the **Connect account** button, as shown in the following screenshot:

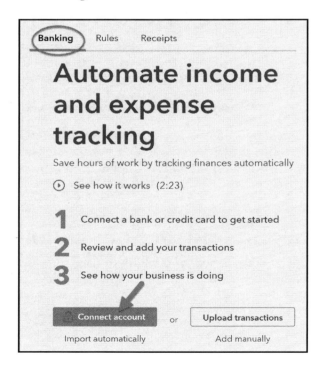

3. To connect your bank account, select your bank by clicking on the icon or typing the name of the bank in the search box, as shown in the following screenshot:

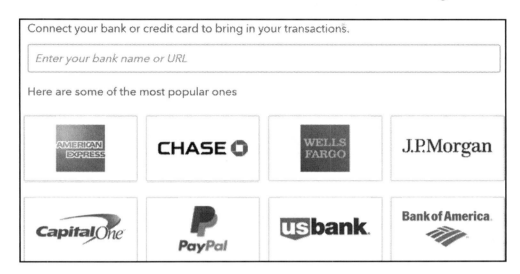

If you cannot locate your bank, you will not be able to connect your account to QuickBooks; however, you can download your banking information into QuickBooks, which we will cover in the next section.

4. You will need to sign in to your bank account using the secure user ID and password issued by your bank:

5. Before connecting your bank account to QBO, you will be required to consent to the terms and conditions set by your bank. This consent confirmation is documentation that proves that you agree to share your financial data with QuickBooks:

← Back | Connect Account Information - Confirm

You have selected the following account information that you want Wells Fargo to connect with Intuit. To confirm, select **Connect My Account Information**. You will then be returned to the 3rd party service.

Cash Accounts

BUSINESS MARKET RATE SAVINGS ...

Terms and Conditions

☑ I have read and accept the <u>Terms and Conditions</u>

Connect My Accounts

Follow the remaining on-screen instructions to connect your bank account to QuickBooks. If you have more than one account with the same financial institution, you will have the option to connect all bank accounts or select specific bank accounts to connect with QuickBooks.

Make sure that you only connect business bank accounts to QuickBooks and not personal bank accounts; otherwise, you will have personal banking activity co-mingled with business transactions, which is not a best practice.

You can save yourself a lot of time by connecting your bank account to QuickBooks so that your transactions automatically download. However, if your bank does not allow you to connect your account, you can still save time by obtaining an Excel CSV file from your bank so that you can upload the transactions to your QuickBooks file.

Uploading banking transactions from an Excel CSV file

If your financial institution does not integrate with QuickBooks, then you need to download your banking transactions to an Excel CSV file. Most banks allow you to download your transactions to a PDF or CSV file. Log into your bank account and look for the **Download Transactions** option. If you don't see this option, contact your bank and inform them that you need your banking transactions in a CSV file so that you can download them to QuickBooks.

To upload banking transactions from an Excel CSV file to QuickBooks, go through the following instructions:

1. At the beginning of this chapter, we showed you how to add a new account to the chart of accounts list. Follow those step-by-step instructions and add your bank account to QuickBooks.

   Your bank account setup screen should resemble the one in the following screenshot:

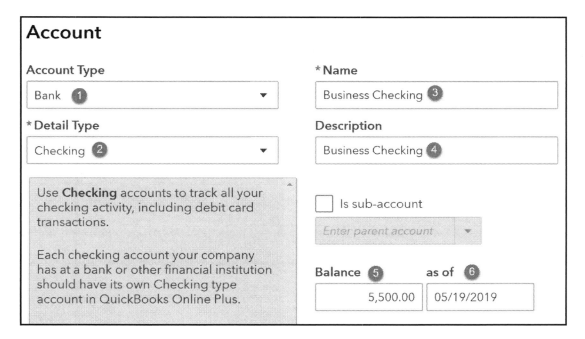

The following is a brief explanation of how to fill in the new bank account fields:

- **Account Type (1)**: The account type will be **Bank** for all checking, savings, and money market accounts.
- **Detail Type (2)**: From the dropdown, select the type of bank account you want to add. Your choices are cash-on-hand, checking, money market, savings, and trust account.
- **Name (3)**: The name of the bank account belongs in this field. In our example, we have created a business checking account and have named it accordingly. This will work if all of your bank accounts are at the same financial institution; however, if you have multiple bank accounts set up at different financial institutions, you should include the name of the bank along with the type of account in this field—for example, *Wells Fargo Business Checking*, *Bank of America Business Savings*, and so on.
- **Description (4)**: You can include a brief description of the account that you are adding in this field.
- **Balance (5)**: Enter the current balance in your bank account as of your QuickBooks start date. For example, if you are starting to use QuickBooks as of January 1, enter the balance of your bank account as of the last day of the previous period, which would be December 31 of the previous year.

It's important to have your bank statements handy as you are adding bank accounts to QuickBooks. This is to ensure that you enter the correct balance and effective dates. If you leave this field blank, you will not be able to access this field later on. Instead, you will have to make a balance adjustment directly in the check register.

- **as of (6)**: Enter the date that the balance is effective from. This information should be identical to the date on the bank statement.

2. From the gear icon, select **Import Data**, which is located in the **Tools** column, as shown in the following screenshot:

3. The import data screen is where you can import banking transactions, customers, vendors, a chart of accounts list, and a products and services list. Select the **Bank Data** option to display the setup screen, as shown in the following screenshot:

4. Before uploading your file, you need to save it in a CSV (.csv) format. Click on the **Browse** button to select the file that you want to upload and the name of the file will appear in the dialog box to the left of the browse button, as shown in the following screenshot:

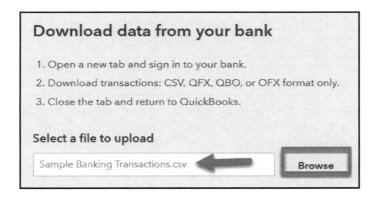

5. In this step, you will select the bank account that you want the bank transactions to upload to in QuickBooks. Select the bank account from the drop-down menu, as shown in the following screenshot:

6. In this step, you will map the columns in your CSV file to a field in QuickBooks. This is a very important step to ensure that the information is entered into the correct fields in QuickBooks. For each QBO field located on the left, select the column where you want the data to appear in your CSV file, as shown in the following screenshot:

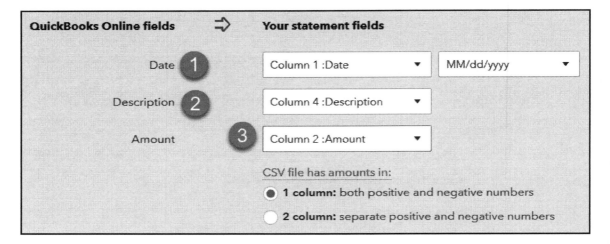

There are three fields that need to be populated in QuickBooks: the transaction date, a brief description, and the transaction amount. You will need to indicate what column in your CSV file includes this information.

The following is a brief description of the information you will need to complete to map the fields in the CSV file to the QBO fields:

- **Date** (1): From the dropdown, select the column in the CSV file that includes the date of the banking transactions. You can also select the format that the date is in (for example, **MM/dd/yyyy**).
- **Description** (2): Select the column in the CSV file that includes a description of the transaction.
- **Amount** (3): From the dropdown, select the column in the CSV file that includes the transaction amount. Amounts can be formatted into one column that includes both positive and negative numbers or into two separate columns, one for positive numbers (withdrawals) and one for negative numbers (deposits) figures.

7. On the screen shown in the following screenshot, you will see how your data will upload to QuickBooks. It's important to review the data to ensure that it is populating the correct fields:

Select the transactions to import

	DATE	DESCRIPTION	AMOUNT
✓	03/20/2017	Parking fees	-10.50
✓	04/04/2017	Tax prep ck5645	-250.00
✓	01/17/2017	Payment	-100.00
✓	02/16/2017	payment	-100.00
✓	03/20/2017	payment	-100.00

If you don't want to upload all transactions, you can remove the checkmark from the first column for any transaction that you do not want to upload to QuickBooks.

8. On the next screen, QuickBooks will provide you with the number of transactions to be uploaded. This is your final opportunity to confirm that the data is correct. Once you confirm, there will be no undo button. To proceed with the upload, click the **Yes** button, as shown in the following screenshot:

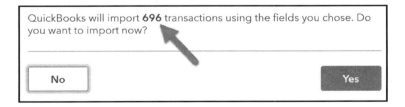

After confirming the number of transactions to import, your transactions will be added to QuickBooks. To confirm, head over to the banking center, where you can see the date, description, and amount of transactions that were successfully imported from your CSV file.

Now that we know how to connect our bank accounts to QBO, let's learn how to connect our credit card accounts in the next section.

Connecting credit card accounts to QuickBooks Online

Similar to bank accounts, you can connect your credit card accounts to QBO. There are two ways that you can update QuickBooks with your credit card activity. You can connect your credit card account to QuickBooks so that transactions import automatically into QuickBooks. The other option is to upload transactions from an Excel spreadsheet. We will walk you through each process in more detail in the following sections.

Importing credit card transactions automatically

There are several benefits to importing your credit card transactions automatically. First, you will save a lot of time because you won't have to manually enter transactions. Second, QuickBooks will be updated on a *daily* basis with the most recent credit card activity on your account. Third, it will be much easier to reconcile your credit card accounts.

The following are the five steps that are required to import credit card transactions automatically into QBO:

1. Select **Banking** from the left menu bar, as shown in the following screenshot:

2. On the following screen, you will see a link to a short video tutorial, which is a demo of how the banking center works. Click on the **Connect account** button as shown in the following screenshot:

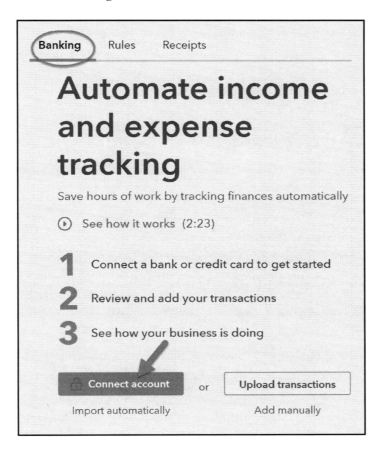

3. To connect your credit card account, select your credit card company by clicking on the icon or typing the name of the financial institution in the search box, as shown in the following screenshot:

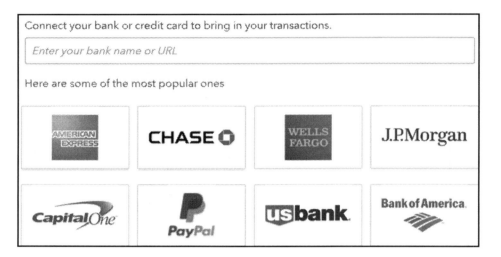

 If you cannot locate your financial institution, you will not be able to connect your account to QuickBooks; however, you can download your credit card transactions into QuickBooks, which we will cover in the next section.

4. You will need to sign in to your credit card account using the secure user ID and password issued by your bank.

5. Before connecting your credit card account to QBO, you will be required to consent to the terms and conditions set by your bank. This consent is documentation proving that you agree to share your financial data with QuickBooks.

Follow the remaining on-screen instructions to connect your credit card account to QuickBooks. If you have more than one account with the same financial institution, you will have the option to connect all credit card accounts or select specific credit card accounts to connect with QuickBooks.

 Make sure that you only connect business credit card accounts to QuickBooks and not personal credit card accounts; otherwise, you will have personal credit card activity comingled with business transactions, which is not ideal.

After connecting your bank accounts to QuickBooks, they will appear in the banking center. From the banking center, you can see the date of the most recent download along with a description and the amount of each transaction downloaded. If your financial institution does not allow you to connect your credit card account to QuickBooks, you will need to upload credit card transactions from an Excel CSV file.

Uploading credit card transactions from an Excel CSV file

If your financial institution does not integrate with QuickBooks, you need to download your credit card transactions to an Excel CSV file. Most banks allow you to download your transactions to a PDF or CSV file. Log into your credit card account and look for the download transactions option. If you don't see this option, contact the credit card company and inform them that you need your transactions in a CSV file so you can download them to QuickBooks.

To upload credit card transactions from an Excel CSV file to QuickBooks, follow these instructions:

1. At the beginning of this chapter, we showed you how to add a new account to the chart of accounts list. Follow those step-by-step instructions and add your credit card account to QuickBooks.
2. Your credit card account setup screen should resemble the one in the following screenshot:

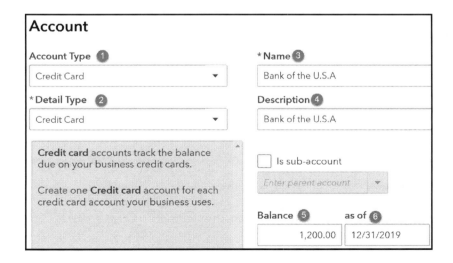

The following is a brief explanation of the new credit card account fields:

- **Account Type** (1): The account type will be **Credit Card**.
- **Detail Type** (2): This field will automatically be populated with your selection for the account type.
- **Name** (3): The name of the credit card belongs in this field. If you have multiple credit card accounts at the same financial institution, you may want to consider entering the last four digits of each account in the account name field. This will make it easier when you are entering transactions and reconciling accounts.
- **Description** (4): You can include a brief description of the account that you are adding in this field or enter the name of the account.
- **Balance** (5): Enter the current outstanding balance due on your credit card account as of your QuickBooks start date. For example, if you began to use QuickBooks as of January 1, enter the balance owed on your credit card as of the last day of the previous period, which would be December 31 of the previous year.
- **as of** (6): Enter the date that the balance is effective from. This information should be identical to the date on the credit card statement. If your balance is zero, then there is no need to complete this field.

It's important to have your credit card statements handy as you are adding credit card accounts to QuickBooks. This is to ensure that you enter the correct balance and effective dates. If you leave this field blank, you will not be able to access this field later on; instead, you will have to make a balance adjustment directly in the credit card register.

3. From the gear icon, select **Import Data** located in the **Tools** column, as shown in the following screenshot:

4. The import data screen is where you can import bank and credit card transactions, customers, vendors, a chart of accounts list, and a products and services list. Select the **Bank Data** option to display the setup screen, as shown in the following screenshot:

5. Before uploading your file, you need to save it in a CSV (.csv) format. Click on the **Browse** button to select the file to upload and the name of the file will appear in the dialog box to the left of the **Browse** button, as shown in the following screenshot:

6. Next, select the credit card account that you want the transactions to upload to in QuickBooks. From the drop-down menu, select the credit card account as indicated in the following screenshot:

7. Map the columns in your CSV file to a field in QuickBooks. This is a very important step to ensure that the information is populated in the correct fields in QuickBooks. For each QBO field located on the left, select the column that the data appears in your CSV file, as shown in the following screenshot:

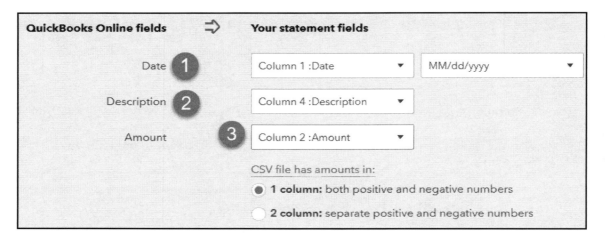

The following is a brief explanation of the new fields that are labeled in the preceding screenshot:

- **Date** (1): From the dropdown, select the column in the CSV file that includes the date of the credit card transactions. You can also select the format that the date is in (for example, **MM/dd/yyyy**).
- **Description** (2): Select the column in the CSV file that includes a description of the transaction.
- **Amount** (3): From the dropdown, select the column in the CSV file that includes the transaction amount. Amounts can be formatted into one column that includes both positive and negative numbers or into two separate columns, one for positive numbers (credit card charges) and one for negative numbers (credit card payments and credits).

8. On this screen, you will see how your data will upload to QuickBooks. It's important to review the data to ensure it is populating the correct fields:

Select the transactions to import

☑	DATE	DESCRIPTION	AMOUNT
☑	03/20/2017	Parking fees	-10.50
☑	04/04/2017	Tax prep ck5645	-250.00
☑	01/17/2017	Payment	-100.00
☑	02/16/2017	payment	-100.00
☑	03/20/2017	payment	-100.00

If you don't want to upload all transactions, you can remove the checkmark from the first column for any transaction you do not want to upload to QuickBooks.

9. On this screen, QuickBooks will provide you with the number of transactions to be uploaded. This is your final opportunity to confirm that the data is correct. Once you confirm this, there is no undo button. To proceed with the upload, click the **Yes** button, as shown in the following screenshot:

After confirming the number of credit card transactions to import, your transactions will be added to QuickBooks. To confirm this, head over to the banking center, where you can see the date, description, and numbers of credit card transactions that were successfully imported from your CSV file.

Now that we know how to connect credit card accounts to QBO, let's see how to provide access to other users in the next section.

Giving other users access to your QuickBooks data

The ability to give other users access to your data is one of the many benefits of using QBO. All QBO subscriptions include access for two accountant users and access for one or more additional users. There are five types of users that you can create in QBO:

- Standard user
- Company administrator
- Reports only
- Time tracking
- Accountant

We will discuss each of these in more detail in the following subsections.

Standard user

You can give the standard user full or limited access to your QBO data, excluding administrative privileges. You can choose to give the standard user full access, access to customers and vendors, access to customers only, or access to vendors only.

Go through the following steps to create a standard user:

1. From the gear icon, select **Manage Users** in the **Your Company** column, as shown in the following screenshot:

2. Click on the **Add user** button, as shown in the following screenshot:

3. Click on **Standard user**, as shown in the following screenshot:

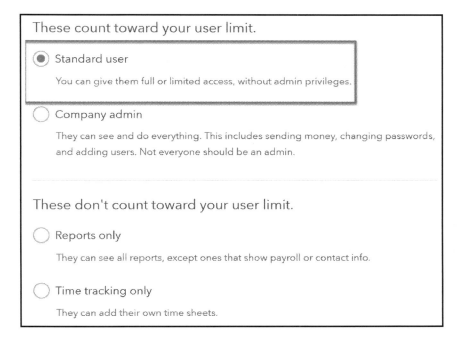

A standard user will count towards the total number of users included in your QBO subscription. If you recall, we covered the total number of users that can be included in each subscription plan.

To recap, the following is a summary of the number of users that are included in each plan:

- **QuickBooks Online Simple Start**: 2 accountants, 1 user
- **QuickBooks Online Essentials**: 2 accountants, 3 users
- **QuickBooks Online Plus**: 2 accountants, 5 users
- **QuickBooks Online Advanced**: 2 accountants, 25 users

4. The following is a snapshot of the access rights you can choose from—**All**, **None**, or **Limited**:

How much access do you want this user to have?	All access

◉ All
◯ None
◯ Limited
  ☐ Customers
  ☐ Vendors
	This user can see and do everything with:
	
	✔ Customers and Sales
	✔ Vendors and Purchases
	
	They can also:
	
	✔ Add, edit, and delete employees
	✔ Change preferences
	✔ View activity log
	✔ Create, edit, and delete budgets
	✔ Add, edit, and delete accounts
	✔ Make deposits and transfer funds
	✔ Reconcile accounts and make journal entries
	✔ View all reports
	✔ Turn on sales tax for the company
	✔ Change the setup for existing sales tax information
	✔ Make sales tax adjustments and file sales tax returns
	✔ Set up multicurrency
	✔ Perform home currency adjustments

All-access rights give the user the ability to manage all customers, sales, vendors, and purchase transactions. Limited access rights allow you to give someone access to customers and/or vendor transactions.

The following is a snapshot of the access rights for **Customers**:

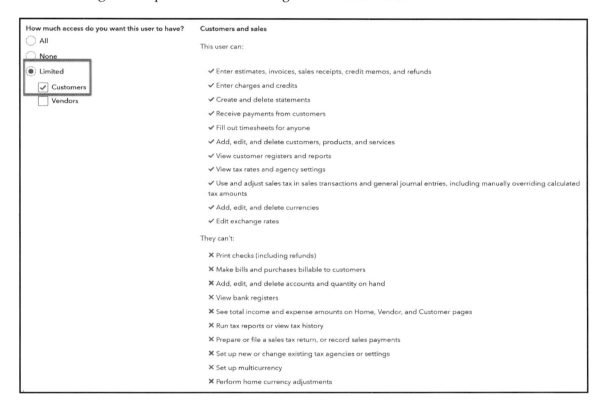

Limited Customer access rights give the user the ability to manage all customers and sales transactions. This level of access would be ideal for an accounts receivable clerk.

The following is a snapshot of the access rights for **Vendors**:

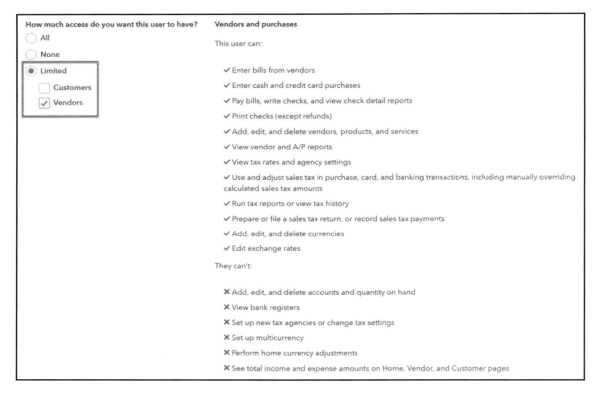

Limited Vendor access rights give the user the ability to manage all vendor and purchasing transactions. This level of access would be ideal for an accounts payable clerk.

The standard user category is ideal for users who need access to customers and vendor transactions. All-access rights are ideal for someone who manages accounts payable or accounts receivable. Limited access to customers is ideal for an accounts receivable clerk who only needs access to customers and sales, whereas limited access to vendors is ideal for an accounts payable clerk who needs access to vendors and purchasing transactions.

Company administrator

The company administrator role includes access to every aspect of QuickBooks. This includes adding new users, changing passwords, and having control of your QBO subscription. Because there are no limitations to what this user can do, we recommend that you limit this role to owners of the business, IT personnel, or an officer of the company. Similar to the standard role, the company administrator role counts toward your user limit. To add a company administrator, follow steps 1 and 2 in the *Standard user* section. In step 3, select **Company administrator** and follow the on-screen prompts to complete the setup.

Reports only user

The reports only role is very limited. This role can generate just about any report in QuickBooks except payroll or vendor and customer contact information; however, the reports only user cannot add, edit, or change any QuickBooks data. They also do not have the ability to view anything outside of reports. This role is ideal for a partner who wants to periodically review reports, but has no day-to-day responsibilities. Unlike the standard and company admin roles, the reports only role does not count toward your user limit, which means you can give reports only access to an unlimited number of users. To add a reports only user, follow steps 1 and 2 in the *Standard user* section. In step 3, select **Reports only** and follow the on-screen prompts to complete the setup.

Time tracking user

Similar to the reports only role, the time tracking user role is also very limited. This role is limited to entering timesheets. It is ideal for employees and contractors who don't need access to any other areas of QuickBooks. Similar to the reports only role, the time tracking user does not count toward your user limit. This means that you can add an unlimited number of time tracking users. To add a time tracking user, follow steps 1 and 2 in the *Standard user* section. In step 3, select **Time tracking only** and follow the on-screen prompts to complete the setup.

Accountant user

Each QBO plan includes two accountants users, at no additional cost. The level of access the accountant user has is identical to that of the company administrator. Accountant users can access all areas of QuickBooks. This includes adding users, editing passwords, and managing your QuickBooks subscription. You should be extremely careful with who you give this level of access to; ideally, it should be limited to your CPA, tax preparer, and bookkeeper.

Go through the following steps to invite an accountant to access your QuickBooks data:

1. Click on the gear icon and select **Manage Users** right after the company info column, as shown in the following screenshot:

2. On the **Manage users** page, click on **Accounting firms**, as shown in the following screenshot:

3. Click on the **Invite** button, as shown in the following screenshot, to invite your accountant to access your QuickBooks data:

4. Enter the name and email address of your accountant, as shown in the following screenshot:

What's your accountant's contact info?

Your accountant and members of their firm will have admin access to your company data.

First name

Crystalynn

Last name

Shelton

Email

mycpa@gmail.com

This will be their user id.

Once you have entered your accountant's contact information, click the **Send** button. Your accountant will receive an email inviting them to access your QBO account. They will need to accept the invitation and create a secure password. Their user ID will be the email address that you entered in the form.

You should now have a better understanding of the five types of users you can set up in QuickBooks (standard, company admin, reports only, time tracking only, and accountant). Using the detailed information we have provided on the level of access each user has, you can start inviting your accountant, bookkeeper, and other users to access your QuickBooks data.

Summary

In this chapter, we showed you how to customize the chart of accounts by adding, editing, and deleting accounts. We covered how to connect your bank and credit card accounts to QuickBooks so that transactions automatically download into QuickBooks. We also covered how to import banking transactions into QuickBooks from a CSV file. Finally, we showed you how to give other users, such as a bookkeeper, partner, or CPA, full or limited access to your QuickBooks data. By now, you should know how to manage your chart of accounts, bank, and credit card accounts, and how to add additional users.

In the next chapter, we will show you how to manage customers, vendors, and products and services in QBO. This will include how to add, edit, and inactivate new customers, vendors, and products and services.

Managing Customers, Vendors, Products, and Services

5

Now that you've created your company files, it's time to add the people you do business with on a regular basis. This includes your customers that you sell your products and services to, and the vendors who you purchase services and supplies from. We will also cover how to create your products and services list in QuickBooks Online so that you can keep track of your sales.

In this chapter, we will cover the following key concepts:

- Managing customers in QuickBooks Online
- Managing vendors in QuickBooks Online
- Managing products and services in QuickBooks Online

By the end of this chapter, you will understand how to add, edit, and delete customers, vendors, and the products and services that you sell.

Managing customers in QuickBooks Online

A customer is anyone that you sell products or services to. A customer can be an individual or a business. Some of the information QuickBooks Online allows you to keep track of for customers is contact information such as their telephone number and email address, payment terms, invoicing, and payment history. You can enter customer information manually or import it from an Excel spreadsheet. We will show you both methods in this section.

Manually adding customers in QuickBooks Online

In order to add new customers to QuickBooks Online (QBO), you need to have the basic contact details about your customer. This includes their company name, billing address, business telephone number, and the first and last name of the primary contact. You should also know what payment terms you will extend to customers (for example, net 30 days, net 60 days, and so on).

Follow these steps to add a new customer in QuickBooks Online:

1. Navigate to **Customers** by selecting **Invoicing** from the left-hand menu bar and then **Customers**, as shown in the following screenshot:

2. Fill in the fields on the next screen, as shown in the following screenshot:

Customer information

Company ①

Email ⑥

George_Jetson@thejetsons.com

Title	First name ②	Middle name	Last name	Suffix
	George		Jetson	

Phone ⑦	Mobile	Fax
(512) 854-1234		

*Display name as

George Jetson ③ ▾

Other ⑧   **Website**

Print on check as ☑ Use display name

☐ Is sub-customer

George Jetson ④

Enter parent customer ▾   Bill with parent ▾

⑤ | ⑩ | ⑪ | ⑫ | ⑬ | ⑭

Address | Notes | Tax info | Payment and billing | Attachments | Additional Info

Billing address map

321 Jetson Drive

Jetson	CA
90210	Country

Shipping address map ☑ Same as billing address

321 Jetson Drive ⑨

Jetson	CA
90210	Country

The following is a brief description of the 14 fields of information you can enter for new customers:

- **Company**: If the customer is a business, you will enter the business name in this field. If the customer is an individual, you will leave this field blank.
- **First** and **Last name**: If the customer is an individual, enter their first and last name in these fields. If the customer is a business, leave this field blank.
- **Display name as**: There is no need to input anything in this field; it will automatically populate with the information you entered in the company name or first and last name fields.
- **Print on check as**: Similar to the **Display name as** field, this field will automatically populate with the information that you entered in the company name or first and last name fields. If you need to change the payee name, simply remove the checkmark above this field and enter the name you would like to appear on checks.

- **Address**: Enter the address where your customers would like their invoices to be mailed to and/or where correspondence should be sent. Even if you plan to email all the invoices and other correspondence, we recommend that you keep an address on file for all of your customers.
- **Email**: Enter the business email address for customers in this field.
- **Phone**: Enter the business telephone number for customers in this field.
- **Other** and **Website**: Enter an additional contact phone number in the **Other** field, along with the company website in the **Website** field.
- **Shipping address**: If the shipping address differs from the billing address, enter the shipping address in this field. Otherwise, ensure that the shipping address is the same as the billing address; then, QuickBooks will automatically populate these fields with the address you entered in the billing address field.
- **Notes**: This field can be used to enter additional information about your customers, such as any preferences they have or even to document previous incidents or issues. This information is for internal use only and is not visible to the customer.
- **Tax info**: If you have customers who are exempt from sales tax, you should request a copy of their resale certificate and enter the resale number in this field. This will cover you if you ever have a sales tax audit and need to provide supporting information on why you did not charge a customer sales tax.
- **Payment and billing**: There are four fields in this section: preferred payment method, preferred delivery method, payment terms, and opening A/R balance.
- **Preferred payment method**: Select the preferred method the customer likes to remit payment. If it's a credit card, you can enter the credit card details and keep them on file for future payments. However, you must be `PCI compliant` when it comes to sensitive information such as this. Let's take a look at the options we have here:
  - **Preferred delivery method**: Select the preferred way the customer likes to receive invoices (for example, US mail or email).
  - **Payment terms**: Select the payment terms for your customer. The most common payment term is net 30, which means invoices are due 30 days after the invoice date. It's important that you select payment terms for all your customers so that QuickBooks can alert you when invoices are due or past due.

- **Opening A/R balance**: Generally, you wouldn't use this field unless converting from other accounting software. This field is useful for recording the existing accounts receivable balance that customers have with you at the time of converting from your old accounting system to QuickBooks. However, if you plan to enter unpaid invoices into QuickBooks, leave this field blank.
- **Attachments**: You can store important documents such as contracts, engagement letters, or proposals in QuickBooks. Simply scan the document into your computer and attach it to the customer it is associated with.
- **Additional info**: There is a field called **Customer Type** in this section. If you need to categorize your customers into different types (for example, wholesaler, retailer, and so on), you can create custom types and assign each customer to a type. This will allow you to run reports and filter by customer type to get detailed information, such as sales by customer type.

We'll learn how to import customers in QBO in the next section.

Importing customers into QuickBooks Online

If you have more than a handful of customers, you may want to consider importing your customers into QuickBooks instead of manually entering them. You can import all of your customer details from a CSV file into QuickBooks.

Follow these steps to import customers into QuickBooks Online:

1. Navigate to **Customers** by selecting **Invoicing** from the left-hand menu bar and then **Customers**, as shown in the following screenshot:

2. Click the drop-down arrow next to the **New customer** button and select **Import customers**, as shown in the following screenshot:

3. Click the **Browse** button to upload the CSV file from your computer, as shown in the following screenshot:

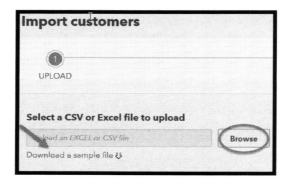

 Download the sample file (shown in the preceding screenshot). This file includes all of the fields of information you can upload for customers. Save this file and use it as your template.

4. Follow the on-screen instructions to import your customer data into QBO.

We will learn how to make changes to existing customers in the next section.

Making changes to existing customers in QuickBooks Online

There may be times when you need to correct or update a customer's information. For example, if a customer's address changes or their primary contact changes, you will need to update your records with the new information. Updating customer information is easy to do in QuickBooks – all you need to do is navigate to the **Customers** center and select the customer that you need to make changes to.

Follow these steps to edit an existing customer in QuickBooks Online:

1. Navigate to **Customers** by selecting **Invoicing** from the left-hand menu bar and then **Customers**, as shown in the following screenshot:

2. Select the customer you would like to edit by clicking on the customer's name, as shown in the following screenshot:

CUSTOMER / PROJECT ▲ / COMPANY	PHONE	OPEN BALANCE
Amy's Bird Sanctuary ✉ Amy's Bird Sanctuary	(650) 555-3311	$239.00
Bill's Windsurf Shop ✉ Bill's Windsurf Shop	(415) 444-6538	$85.00
Cool Cars ✉ Cool Cars	(415) 555-9933	$0.00
Diego Rodriguez ✉	(650) 555-4477	$0.00

3. The detailed customer record will be displayed on the next screen. Click on the **Customer Details** tab and then the **Edit** button to make changes:

You can update the information you have on file for your customers at any time. Having up-to-date information will ensure that invoices, sales receipts, and other documents have the most recent contact information, such as billing and shipping address information, on file.

Inactivating customers in QuickBooks Online

As we mentioned previously, you cannot delete customers, vendors, or products once you have used them in a transaction. However, you can inactivate customers, vendors, and products, which will keep the existing transactions recorded in QuickBooks, but "hide" the customer, vendor, or item from the drop-down list.

Follow these steps to inactivate customers in QuickBooks Online:

1. Navigate to **Customers** by selecting **Invoicing** from the left-hand menu bar and then **Customers**, as shown in the following screenshot:

2. Put a checkmark next to the customer you want to inactivate and select **Make inactive**, as shown in the following screenshot:

As we mentioned previously, you can inactivate customers, vendors, and items that have been used in a transaction from their drop-down lists. This action is called **Inactivate** and it will prevent someone from selecting customers, vendors, and items you no longer wish to use, while preserving the historical transactions that have been recorded for each customer, vendor, and item at the same time.

Managing vendors in QuickBooks Online

A vendor is an individual or a business that you pay. Vendors can be 1099 contractors, a utility company, or a business you purchase products from. Similar to customers, you can keep track of all vendor information such as company address, telephone number, email address, and federal tax ID number for 1099 reporting. 1099 reporting is required for contractors who you have paid $600 or more to within a calendar year. In this section, we will show you how to add new vendors, edit existing vendors, and inactivate vendors in QuickBooks.

Manually adding vendors in QuickBooks Online

To add new vendors to QBO, you need to have each vendor's contact details. This includes a business telephone number, remit to address, email address, and tax ID number (or social security number) for 1099 vendors. You can also enter the payment terms your vendor has extended to you. Entering these payment terms will allow QuickBooks to remind you when bills are due or past due.

Follow these steps to manually add vendors in QuickBooks Online:

1. Navigate to **Vendors** by clicking on **Expenses** on the left-hand menu bar and selecting **Vendors**, as shown in the following screenshot:

2. Click the **New vendor** button, as shown in the following screenshot:

3. Fill in the fields in the new vendor window, as shown in the following screenshot:

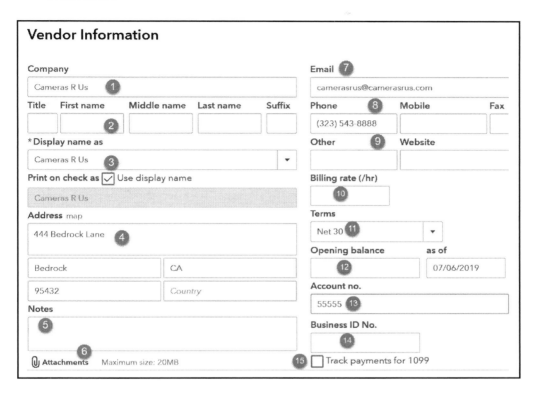

The following is a brief description of the 15 fields of information you can enter for new vendors:

- **Company**: Enter the name of the business that you are purchasing from. If the vendor is an individual, such as a **1099** contractor, leave this field blank and complete the first and last name fields instead.
- **First name** and **Last name**: Enter the name of the individual you are purchasing goods or services from.
- **Display name as**: QuickBooks will automatically populate this field with the information that was entered in either the company field or the first and last name fields.
- **Address**: Enter the address where you send payments to.

If you make your payments online or via credit card, it's still a good idea to keep an address on file for each vendor. This is especially important to do for 1099 contractors because you are required to mail a 1099 form to them at the end of the year for tax reporting purposes.

- **Notes**: This field can be used to record internal notes about vendors.
- **Attachments**: Similar to customers, you can attach key vendor documents to a vendor record, such as proposals, contracts, a W9 form, or any other documents.
- **Email address**: Enter the primary email address for the vendor in this field. This email address will be used to send purchase orders and other vendor-related documents directly from QuickBooks.
- **Phone**: Enter the business telephone number, cellphone, and fax number in these fields.
- **Other** and **Website**: Use the **Other** field to enter any additional information you would like to keep track of. If the vendor has a website, enter that information here as well.
- **Billing rate**: If you have an agreed-upon billing rate that does not change, enter that information in this field. However, if the billing rate varies, leave this field blank.
- **Payment terms**: Select the payment terms the vendor has extended to you (for example, net 30 days, net 15 days, or due upon receipt). It's important to select payment terms so that QuickBooks can use this information to remind you when bills are due or past due.
- **Opening balance**: If you are converting from another accounting software to QuickBooks, you can enter the outstanding accounts payable balance for suppliers in this field. However, if you plan to manually enter unpaid bills into QuickBooks, leave this field blank.
- **Account number**: If your vendor has given you an account number, enter it into this field. Otherwise, you can leave this field blank.
- **Business ID Number**: Enter the social security number or federal tax ID number for all 1099 vendors in this field. If a business is incorporated, there is no need to obtain this information.

It's good practice to request a W9 form from all 1099 contractors before you remit payment. A W9 form includes the individual's first and last name, their company name (DBA), mailing address, business entity (for example, sole prop, LLC, and so on), and social security or federal tax ID number. This form will give you all of the information you need to add them to QuickBooks as a new vendor and complete 1099 reporting at the end of the year.

- **Track payments for 1099**: Select this checkbox for any individuals you purchase goods and services from that are not incorporated. By marking this box, QuickBooks will flag these vendors so that they appear on the 1099 report at the end of the year.

If you pay $600 or more to a 1099 contractor during the year, you are required to provide each contractor with a 1099 form at the end of the year. If total payments during the year do not equal $600 or more, you are not required to provide a 1099 form.

Similar to customers, you can include a wealth of information in QuickBooks about your vendors. By including this information in QuickBooks, you can easily create purchase orders, bills, and other forms and documents without the need to enter this information over and over.

Importing vendors into QuickBooks Online

If you have more than a few vendors to add to QuickBooks, you may want to consider importing the information instead of manually inputting it into QuickBooks. Similar to customers, you can import your vendor details from a CSV file.

Follow these steps to import vendors into QuickBooks Online:

1. Navigate to **Vendors** by clicking on **Expenses** on the left-hand menu bar and selecting **Vendors**, as shown in the following screenshot:

2. Click on the arrow to the right of the **New vendor** button and select **Import vendors**, as shown in the following screenshot:

3. Click the **Browse** button to upload the CSV file from your computer, as shown in the following screenshot:

Download the sample file (shown in the preceding screenshot). This file includes all of the fields of information you can upload for vendors. Save this file and use it as your template.

4. Follow the on-screen prompts to import your vendors into QBO.

The next section shows how you can make changes to existing vendors.

Making changes to existing vendors in QuickBooks Online

Similar to customers, the information that you have on file for vendors can change. For example, the remit to address where payments are mailed could change or the telephone number may need to be updated. When it does, you can quickly update your records in QuickBooks. You will need to navigate to the **Vendors** center and select the vendor that you need to make changes to.

Follow these steps to edit an existing vendor in QuickBooks Online:

1. Navigate to **Vendors** by clicking on **Expenses** on the left-hand menu bar and selecting **Vendors**, as shown in the following screenshot:

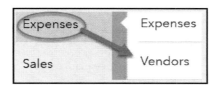

2. Select the vendor you want to edit by clicking on the vendor's name, as shown in the following screenshot:

VENDOR ▲ / COMPANY	PHONE	EMAIL	OPEN BALANCE
Bob's Burger Joint			$0.00
Books by Bessie ✉ Books by Bessie	(650) 555-7745	Books@Intuit.com	$0.00
Brosnahan Insurance Agency	(650) 555-9912		$241.23

3. The detailed vendor record will be displayed on the next screen. Click on the **Vendor Details** tab and then on the **Edit** button to make changes:

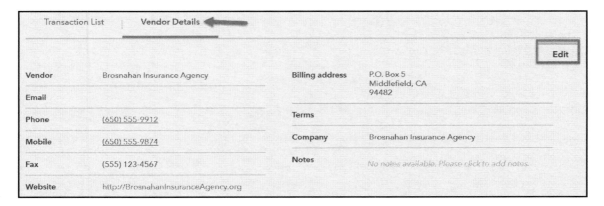

QuickBooks makes it easy to update vendor contact information. Having up-to-date vendor information will ensure all purchase orders, bills, and reports are accurate. If you decide you no longer want to do business with a vendor, but you have existing transactions in QuickBooks, you can inactivate vendors. We will look at this next.

Inactivating vendors in QuickBooks Online

Similar to customers, you can inactivate vendors you no longer do business with. This will maintain your existing vendor transactions that were previously recorded but remove the vendor from the vendor center.

Follow these steps to inactivate vendors in QuickBooks Online:

1. Navigate to **Vendors** by clicking on **Expenses** on the left-hand menu bar and selecting **Vendors**, as shown in the following screenshot:

2. Put a checkmark in the box next to the vendor you want to inactivate and select **Make inactive**, as shown in the following screenshot:

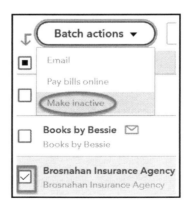

As we mentioned previously, you cannot delete vendors but you can inactivate them. Deactivating a vendor in QuickBooks will preserve the existing historical transactions but remove the vendor from the drop-down list for use in future transactions, such as purchase orders and bills.

Managing products and services in QuickBooks Online

The products and services that you sell are referred to as items in QuickBooks. You can track all of the products and services that you sell in QuickBooks Online. This includes product name, product (item) number, product description, cost, selling price, and quantity on-hand. In this section, we will cover how to manually add items, how to import items, how to modify existing items, and how to inactivate items in QuickBooks Online.

How to manually add products and services in QuickBooks Online

In order to add products and services in QuickBooks, you need to have a list of the products or services you plan to sell, along with the cost, sales price, and a brief description that you want to appear on invoices.

Follow these steps to add a new item in QuickBooks Online:

1. Navigate to the **Products and Services** list by clicking on the gear icon and selecting **Products and Services**, as shown in the following screenshot:

2. On the next screen, you will select the appropriate item type, as shown in the following screenshot:

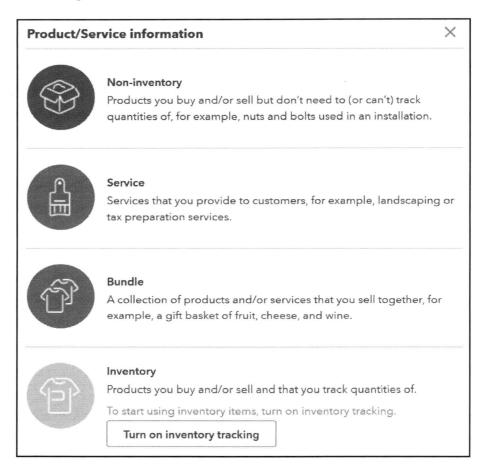

There are four item types to choose from. A brief description of each item type follows:

- **Non-inventory**: The non-inventory type is used to track items you sell but don't keep in inventory. For example, a photographer may purchase photo paper to print pictures but does not keep track of the quantity of photo paper they've purchased.
- **Service**: Service is typically used for services that you sell; for example, bookkeeping services, photography services, or landscaping.
- **Bundle**: A bundle is a collection of products that are sold together; for example, a gift set that includes all of the James Bond movies.

- **Inventory**: Products that you buy and sell and want to track in inventory should be set up as inventory items; for example, a retail T-shirt store that purchases T-shirts and resells them or a grocery store that needs to keep track of the items they've purchased and sold.

 If you want to keep track of the items in your inventory, you will have to turn the inventory feature on. To do so, simply click the **Turn on inventory tracking** button, as shown in the following screenshot:

3. Fill in the following fields to add a new **Service** item:

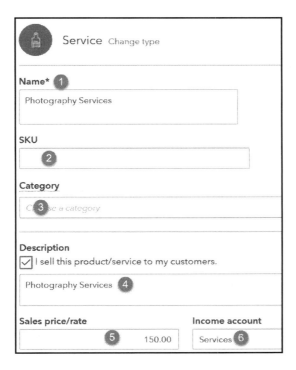

A brief description of the six fields you will complete to add a new **service item** in QuickBooks Online follows:

- **Name**: Enter the name of the product or service you will be selling to customers.
- **SKU**: If applicable, enter the SKU for the product you are selling. In general, a SKU applies to products and not service items.
- **Category**: This field is *optional*. If you want to categorize the products and services you sell, you can do so by creating categories. For example, if you sell T-shirts in three different colors –red, blue, and green – you could create a category for each color to track the sales separately.
- **Description**: Enter a brief description of the item in this field. This description will appear on all customer invoices and sales receipts.
- **Sales price/rate**: Enter the sales price for the item if it generally is the same for all customers. However, if the price varies by customer, you can leave this field blank and complete it when you create an invoice to bill your customers.
- **Income account**: This is a required field. From the dropdown, select the appropriate income account you want sales information about for the item to be recorded on the financial statements.

Every item you create in QuickBooks will be mapped to an account. Using this information, QuickBooks will record the debits and credits for you in the background so that you don't have to.

4. Fill in the following fields to set up an **Inventory** item:

A brief description of the fields you will fill in when setting up an **Inventory** item is as follows:

- **SKU**: A unique number that's used to identify items when they are purchased or sold.
- **Category**: A category is used to group similar items together. In the preceding example, the blue category has been created to group small, medium, and large-size T-shirts together.
- **Quantity on hand**: This should represent the total quantity for each item you have in your inventory.

 You need to perform a physical inventory count before setting up inventory items in QuickBooks Online. If you don't have the inventory quantity when setting up the item, you won't be able to add it to this screen later on. Instead, you will have to create an inventory adjustment journal to record the inventory.

- **As of date**: Enter the date the inventory was counted.
- **Reorder point**: The reorder point is the minimum you want your inventory count to go to before QuickBooks alerts you to place an order. In our example, when the inventory goes down to five T-shirts, QuickBooks will alert us to place an order.
- **Inventory asset account**: All our inventory is recorded as an asset and the default account is **Inventory Asset**, as indicated in our example.

We will learn how to import products and services in the next section.

How to import products and services in QuickBooks Online

Similar to customers and vendors, you can import a products and services list in QuickBooks. This can save you a lot of time if you have a sizeable list of products or services that you sell. You can import this information from a CSV file into QBO.

Follow these steps to import products and services into QuickBooks Online:

1. Navigate to the **Products and Services** list by clicking on the gear icon and selecting **Products and Services**, as shown in the following screenshot:

2. Click on the arrow next to the **New** item button and click on **Import**, as shown in the following screenshot:

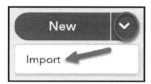

3. Click the **Browse** button to upload the CSV file from your computer, as shown in the following screenshot:

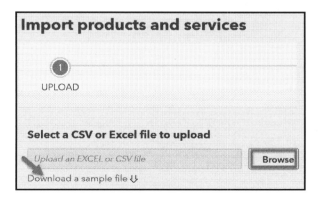

Download the sample file (shown in the preceding screenshot). This file includes all of the fields of information you can upload for items. Save this file and use it as your template.

4. Follow the on-screen prompts to import your products and services into QuickBooks Online.

Now, let's learn how to make changes to existing products and services.

Making changes to existing products and services in QuickBooks Online

You can change any fields in existing products and services except the item type. If you have already used an item in a transaction, QuickBooks will not allow you to change the item type. Instead, you will need to inactivate the old item and add a brand new item with the correct item type.

Follow these steps to make changes to existing products and services in QBO:

1. Navigate to the **Products and Services** list by clicking on the gear icon and selecting **Products and Services**, as shown in the following screenshot:

2. Select the product or service you would like to make changes to by clicking on the name and making the necessary changes, as shown in the following screenshot:

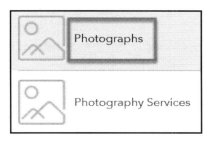

As we mentioned previously, you can change an item type if you haven't used it in a transaction in QuickBooks. However, if you have used an item in a transaction and the item type is incorrect, you will need to create a new item with the correct item type and inactivate the old item. We will discuss how to inactivate products and services next.

Inactivating products and services in QuickBooks Online

As we discussed when we talked about customers and vendors, you cannot delete products and services once you have used them in a transaction. However, you can inactivate them. This will preserve the existing transactions and remove the product or service from the items list.

Follow these steps to inactivate a product or service in QuickBooks Online:

1. Navigate to the **Products and Services** list by clicking on the gear icon and selecting **Products and Services**, as shown in the following screenshot:

2. Scroll down the items list to the product (or service), click on the **Edit** button, and select **Make inactive**, as shown in the following screenshot:

Similar to customers and vendors, inactivating a product or service will remove it from selection for future transactions. However, the existing data will remain intact to ensure reports are accurate for tax and other reporting purposes.

Summary

In this chapter, we covered how to add, edit, and inactivate customers, vendors, and products and services (that is, items) in QuickBooks Online. By now, you should know how to manage your customers, vendors, and products and services lists. Now that you have added your customers, it's time to learn how to record your income.

In the next chapter, we will show you how to record sales transactions. This will include entering invoices and sales receipts, applying for customer payments, making deposits, and recording credit memos for customer refunds or exchanges.

6
Recording Sales Transactions in QuickBooks Online

In Chapter 5, *Managing Customers, Vendors, Products, and Services*, you learned how to customize QuickBooks by adding customers, vendors, and the products and services you sell to QuickBooks. Now that you have completed your QuickBooks setup, it's time to learn how to record transactions. In this chapter, we will focus on recording sales transactions in QuickBooks Online. We will cover the three types of sales transactions, when you should use each, how to record each transaction, and the behind-the-scenes accounting that QuickBooks does for you. We will also show you how to record customer payments, and how to issue credit memos and refunds to customers. Recording sales transactions will allow you to keep track of how much money your business is making. This information is important and will help you to determine whether or not your business is profitable.

In this chapter, we will cover the following key concepts:

- Entering sales forms—sales receipts, deposits, and sales invoices
- Recording payments received from customers
- Issuing credit memos and refunds to customers

Understanding sales forms

Recording income for a business can be accomplished in a variety of ways. There are three primary ways to record income in QuickBooks Online. First, a sales receipt is used when you receive payment at the same time you provide products and/or services to your customers. Second, you can use a deposit to record income for a specific customer or to record income from multiple customers at any one time. Third, you can use a sales invoice, which allows you to bill a specific customer, who will pay you based on payment terms that are agreed upon upfront.

In this section, we will cover when and how to record income using a sales receipt, a deposit, and a sales invoice. We will also show you the accounting that takes place behind the scenes for each transaction. This will include the debits and credits recorded for each transaction.

Recording income using a sales receipt

A sales receipt is used when the sale of a product or service and receipt of the customer payment take place simultaneously. For example, retail businesses such as restaurants or a clothing store will receive payment at the same time they provide their service (for example, serving food to customers) or products (for example, providing clothing items for purchase). You can record a sales receipt in QuickBooks by completing a couple of simple steps.

Follow these steps to record a sales receipt:

1. Navigate to the Quick Create menu and select **Sales Receipt**, as indicated in the following screenshot:

2. The following screenshot shows a snapshot of a completed sales receipt, along with a brief description of what to include in each field:

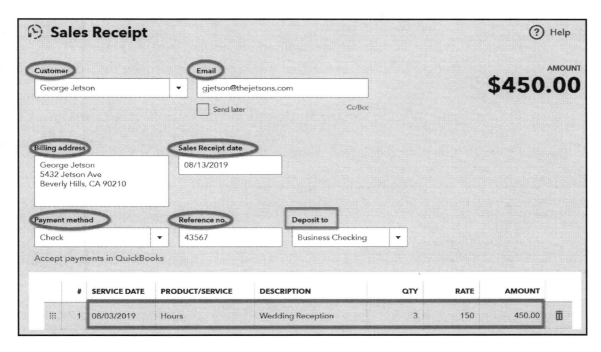

There are several fields of information that need to be completed on the **Sales Receipt** form. In the preceding screenshot, we have highlighted the fields that are mandatory.

The following is a brief description of the information you need to include in each field of the sales receipt:

- **Customer**: Select the customer you sold the product or service to by clicking on the drop-down arrow in this field. If you have not added any customers yet, you can add a new customer by typing the customer name in this field.
- **Email**: This field will automatically populate with the email address you have on file for the customer. If it is blank, you can type an email address directly in this field. QuickBooks will email the sales receipt to the email address you include in this field.
- **Billing address**: This field will automatically populate with the billing address you have on file for this customer. If you don't have an address on file, you can enter one directly in this field.
- **Sales Receipt date**: Enter the date of the sale in this field.

- **Payment method**: Select the payment method by clicking the drop-down arrow.
- **Reference no**: If your customer paid by check, enter the check number in this field. If payment was made by cash or credit card, you can enter a reference number, or leave this field blank.
- **Deposit to**: From the drop-down menu, select the bank account to which you will deposit this payment.
- **SERVICE DATE**: Enter the date of the service or the ship date of the product sold.
- **PRODUCT/SERVICE**: From the drop-down menu, select the type of service (or product) sold to the customer.
- **DESCRIPTION**: This field will automatically populate, based on the product/service selected.
- **QTY**: Enter the quantity of items sold or the total hours of service provided.
- **RATE**: Enter the hourly rate for your services or the unit cost of the product sold.
- **AMOUNT**: You don't need to enter anything in this field. QuickBooks will multiply the quantity by the rate to automatically calculate the total amount of the sales receipt.

As mentioned in Chapter 1, *Getting Started with QuickBooks Online* one of the benefits of using QuickBooks is that you don't need to have knowledge of debits and credits to use the software. QuickBooks will automatically debit and credit the appropriate accounts for you. However, it is important for you to understand the impact of recording transactions in QuickBooks.

The following screenshot shows the journal entry that is recorded behind the scenes in QuickBooks for the sales receipt displayed previously:

Date	Account Name	Debit	Credit
8/13/2019	Business Checking	450	
	Service Income		450

When you create a sales receipt in QuickBooks, it has an impact on the balance sheet and the income statement. In our example, the checking account is increased by $450, which increases the total assets on the balance sheet report. Income is also increased by $450, which increases the total income on profit and loss (the income statement). Now that you know how to use a sales receipt to record income, we will show you how to record income using a deposit, and the impact deposits have on financial statements.

Recording income using a deposit

Another method used to record income in QuickBooks is that of a deposit. The downside to using this method is that you won't have a detailed record of the type of service that was performed since there is no field to select the service or product provided. This method should be used if you don't need to record your sales by the type of product or service that was sold. You can record a lump-sum deposit amount for multiple sales, or you can record deposits for a specific customer. Recording a deposit in QuickBooks can be done in just a couple of steps.

Follow these steps to record income in QuickBooks using a deposit:

1. From the Quick Create menu, select **Bank Deposit** in the **Other** column, as indicated in the following screenshot:

2. The following screenshot shows a snapshot of the **Bank Deposit** form, along with a brief description of what to include in each field:

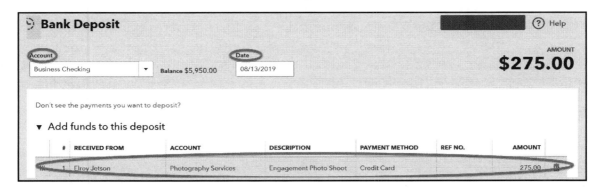

Brief descriptions of the fields that need to be completed in a deposit slip are given here:

- **Account**: Use the drop-down arrow to select the bank account to which the deposit will be made.
- **Date**: Enter the date on which you will make the deposit with your bank.
- **RECEIVED FROM**: Click in this field, and select the customer you received payment from. If you prefer not to track income by the customer, you can leave this field blank.
- **ACCOUNT**: From the drop-down menu, select the appropriate account to which this income should be categorized. This should be based on the type of product or service provided.
- **DESCRIPTION**: This field is optional. You can type a brief description of the product or service provided.
- **PAYMENT METHOD**: In this field, you can indicate the method of payment received (that is, by credit card, cash, or check).
- **REF NO.**: If the payment method was check, enter the check number in this field. For all other payment methods, you can leave this field blank.
- **AMOUNT**: Enter the amount of the sale in this field.

When you create a deposit transaction in QuickBooks, it affects the balance sheet and profit and loss (income statement) reports. The bank account where the deposit will be made goes up, which increases the assets section of the balance sheet report. The profit and loss report is increased by the product or service that was sold.

The following screenshot shows the journal entry recorded for the deposit transaction displayed previously:

Date	Account Name	Debit	Credit
8/13/2019	Business Checking	275	
	Service Income		275

In our example, the business checking account increased by $275, which will increase the total assets on the balance sheet report. Service income also increased by $275, which will increase the total income on the profit and loss (income statement). Now that you know how to record income using a deposit, we will show you how to record income using a sales invoice.

Recording income using a sales invoice

A sales invoice is used to record income from customers who have been given extended payment terms. This means the customer does not pay at the time the product is sold or services are rendered; instead, they pay you sometime in the future. The most common payment term is net 30, which means the invoice is due 30 days from the sales date or the invoice date.

Unlike the sales receipt and deposit form which records both the sale and the receipt of payment in one transaction, recording a sales invoice and payment is done in two steps. In this section, we will cover the first step—recording a sales invoice. We will cover recording customer payments in the next section.

To record a sales invoice in QuickBooks Online, follow these steps:

1. Navigate to the Quick Create menu and select **Invoice** under **Customers**, as indicated here:

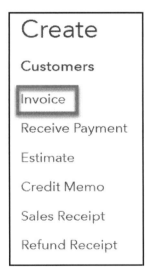

2. The following screenshot shows a snapshot of the sales invoice form, along with example of what information should be included:

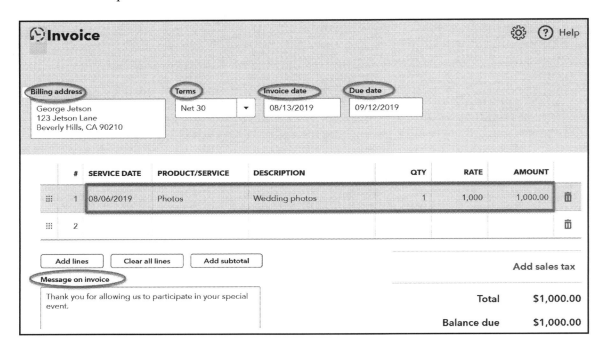

Here are brief descriptions of the fields that need to be completed in a sales invoice:

- **Billing address**: This field will automatically populate with the address information you have on file for your customer. If you have not set up the address information, you can type it directly in this field.
- **Terms**: This field will automatically populate with the payment terms you have set up for your customer. In our example, we have set payment terms of **Net 30,** which means the invoice is due 30 days from the invoice date. If you have not set up payment terms, you can select these from the drop-down menu.
- **Invoice date**: Enter the date of the sale in this field.
- **Due date**: This field is automatically calculated by QuickBooks. It adds 30 days to the invoice date in order to compute the date payment is due.

- **SERVICE DATE**: Select the date on which you provided the goods and/or services to your customer.
- **PRODUCT/SERVICE**: From the drop-down menu, select the product and/or services provided to the customer.
- **DESCRIPTION**: This field will automatically populate, based on the product/service selected in the previous field.
- **QTY**: Enter the quantity of the product, or the total hours to bill the customer.
- **RATE**: This field will automatically populate, based on the product/service selected. However, if you don't have a rate set up, you can enter the price per unit or the hourly rate in this field.
- **AMOUNT**: QuickBooks will automatically calculate the total invoice amount by taking the quantity and multiplying it by the rate.
- **Message on invoice**: This field is optional. You can type a personal thank you message to your customer and it will appear on the invoice.

You have the option to print, email, or save the sales invoice as a PDF document. If you would like to allow customers to pay their invoices online, you can sign up for the **Intuit Payments** service. This service allows you to accept payments from customers via credit card, debit card, or ACH bank transfer.

When you create a sales invoice in QuickBooks, it has an impact on the balance sheet and the profit and loss statement. The accounts receivable account will increase, which will result in an increase in the total assets on the balance sheet report. Income will also increase on the profit and loss statement.

The following screenshot shows the journal entry that will be recorded in QuickBooks for our sample sales invoice shown previously:

Date	Account Name	Debit	Credit
8/13/2019	Accounts Receivable	1000	
	Service Income		1000

The amount owed by customers—also known as accounts receivable—goes up by $1,000, and service income is increased by $1,000. In the next section, we will show you how to apply payments to open accounts receivable balances. Now that you know how to record income using a sales invoice, we will cover the second step, which is receiving customer payments. You must correctly apply customer payments to outstanding sales invoices to ensure your accounts receivable balance is always up to date.

Recording customer payments

If you record income using a sales invoice, you will receive payment based on the terms you have agreed with your customer. When customer payments are received, you must apply payments to an outstanding sales invoice in order to reduce the accounts receivable balance.

Follow these steps to receive payment from a customer:

1. Navigate to **Receive Payment**, located below **Customers**, as indicated in the following screenshot:

2. Complete the fields, as indicated in the following screenshot, to record the customer payment:

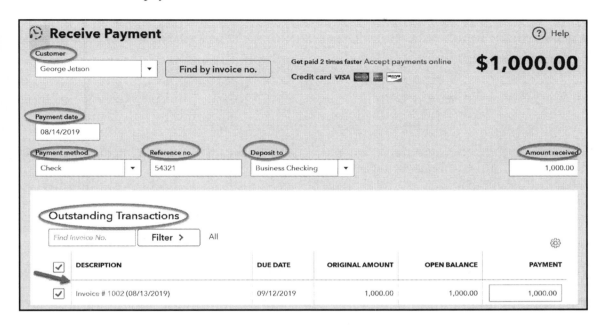

The following are brief descriptions of the key fields for receiving customer payments:

- **Customer**: Select the customer by clicking the drop-down arrow.
- **Payment date**: Enter the date payment was received.
- **Payment method**: From the drop-down menu, select the payment method received (that is, by credit card, check, or cash).
- **Reference no**: If payment was made by check, enter the check number in this field. If another payment method was used, you can leave this field blank.
- **Deposit to**: Select the bank account to which you will deposit this payment.
- **Amount received**: Enter the amount of the payment received.
- **Outstanding Transactions**: A list of unpaid invoices will appear in this section. Based on the amount entered in the **Amount received** field, QuickBooks will select the invoice that matches that amount and is closest to the date of the transaction. In our example shown in the preceding screenshot, there is only one unpaid invoice of $1,000.

Recording customer payments affects the balance sheet report but not the income statement. Since income was recorded at the time the invoice was created, there is no impact on profit and loss (income statement).

The following screenshot shows the journal entry that will be recorded in QuickBooks for a customer payment of $1,000:

Date	Account Name	Debit	Credit
8/14/2019	Business Checking	1000	
	Accounts Receivable		1000

The business checking account is increased by $1,000, which will result in an increase in the assets section of the balance sheet report. Accounts receivable will decrease by $1,000, which will result in a decrease in the assets section of the balance sheet report. Now that you know how to record income and apply payments to outstanding customer invoices, we will show you how to handle customer returns and refunds in the next section.

Issuing credit memos and refunds to customers

There may be times when a customer will return merchandise, or you will need to refund a customer due to an issue with the services you have provided. When that happens, you can create a credit memo in QuickBooks that can be applied to a future invoice, or you can refund the customer their money instead.

Follow these steps to create a credit memo in QuickBooks Online:

1. Click on the Quick Create menu and select **Credit Memo** below **Customers**, as indicated in the following screenshot:

2. Complete the key fields indicated here for the credit memo:

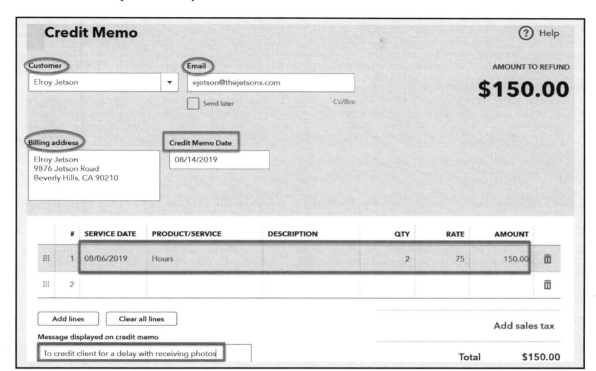

The following are brief descriptions of the key fields to complete for a credit memo:

- **Customer**: From the drop-down menu, select the customer you need to refund.
- **Email**: This field will automatically populate with the email address you have on file. If you don't have an email address on file, you can enter the email address in this field if you would like to email the credit memo to the customer.
- **Billing address**: This field will automatically populate with the billing address you have on file. If you don't have a billing address on file, you can enter it directly in this field.
- **Credit Memo Date**: Enter the date for which you are creating this credit memo.
- **SERVICE DATE**: Enter the date the product or service being refunded was provided.
- **PRODUCT/SERVICE**: From the drop-down menu, select the product or service for which you are providing a refund.
- **DESCRIPTION**: This field will automatically populate, based on the product/service selected.

- **QTY**: Enter the number of items or hours for which you are refunding the customer.
- **RATE**: This field will automatically populate, based on the product/service selected. However, if there is no rate set up, you can enter the rate in this field.
- **Amount**: This field is automatically calculated by multiplying the quantity by the rate. You do not have to enter anything in this field.
- **Message displayed on credit memo**: In this field, you can notate the original invoice number for which you are providing a full or partial credit, along with any additional information you would like to include for the customer.

Recording a credit memo in QuickBooks will have an impact on the balance sheet and income statement reports. The income account will decrease, which will reduce the total income on the profit and loss report. The bank account will also go down because you are refunding money back to the customer. Reducing the bank account will reduce the total assets on the balance sheet report.

The journal entry for the preceding credit memo will be recorded in QuickBooks as follows:

Date	Account Name	Debit	Credit
8/14/2019	Service Income	150	
	Business Checking		150

In our example, service income is reduced by $150, which will decrease the total income on the profit and loss report. In addition, the business checking account has also been reduced by $150, which will be refunded back to the customer.

Summary

In this chapter, you have learned how to record sales transactions using a sales receipt, a deposit, and a sales invoice. You now know when to use each sales transaction, and how to record them in QuickBooks Online. We have also covered the journal entry recorded behind the scenes by QuickBooks for each transaction. In addition, you have learned how to record customer payments so that they are correctly applied to open invoices, and how to issue credit memos and refunds to customers. In the next chapter, we will look at how to record the money that flows out of your business to cover expenses.

7
Recording Expenses in QuickBooks Online

Managing expenses incurred by a business is one of the primary reasons why many businesses decide to use QuickBooks. Most businesses know when they are generating income, but when it comes to where their money is going, it's a whole different story. For a business to be profitable, it must be able to control expenses that directly affect the bottom line. By the end of this chapter, you will know all of the different ways to track your expenses in QuickBooks. Using one or more of these methods will give you access to detailed reports that will give you insight into where you are spending your money. This is a key component in having the ability to control expenses.

In this chapter, we will cover the following topics:

- Entering and paying bills
- Managing recurring expenses
- Writing checks
- Printing checks

Entering and paying bills

Entering bills into QuickBooks and paying them a few days before they become due is the best way to manage your cash flow. If you enter bills into QuickBooks as you receive them, you can run reports that will show you which bills are due or are nearly due so that you can plan ahead, to ensure you have sufficient cash on hand to pay them. Unpaid bills are also referred to as accounts payable, or A/P for short. First, we will cover how to enter bills, and then we will discuss how to pay a bill in **QuickBooks Online** (QBO).

Entering bills into QuickBooks Online

Entering your bills into QuickBooks before they become due will help you to manage your cash flow. You can easily run reports, such as the unpaid bills report or the A/P aging report, to see which bills are becoming due or are past due.

To enter bills into QuickBooks Online, you will need to complete the following steps:

1. Navigate to the Quick Create menu and select **Bill** listed in the **Vendors** column, as indicated in the following screenshot:

2. Complete the key fields in the **Bill** form, as indicated in the following screenshot:

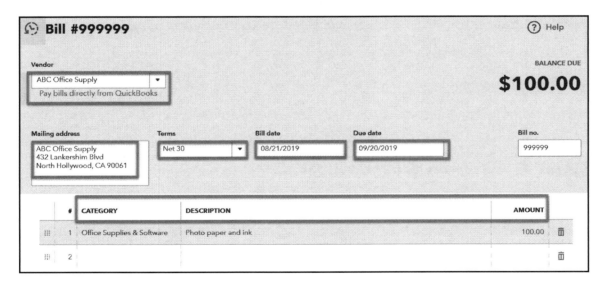

The following is a brief description of the key fields in the **Bill** form:

- **Vendor**: Select a vendor from the drop-down menu, or add a new vendor if they have not been previously set up in QuickBooks.
- **Mailing address**: This field will automatically populate for vendors you have previously created in QuickBooks. If this is a new vendor, you can enter the address in this field.
- **Terms**: This field will automatically populate with the vendor terms you have set up. If you have not previously set up vendor terms, you can select the appropriate payment terms from the drop-down menu.
- **Bill date**: Enter the date that appears on the vendor bill.
- **Due date**: The due date will be calculated automatically, based on the payment terms selected. If payment terms were not selected, you can also enter the due date directly in this field.

When you complete a **Bill** form in QuickBooks, it has an impact on the balance sheet and the profit and loss (income statement) reports. A/P increases, which in turn increases current liabilities on the balance sheet report, expenses on the income statement for non-product purchases, and inventory on the balance sheet report, if you purchased a product for resale.

The journal entry that is recorded in QuickBooks for the preceding bill is shown in the following screenshot:

Date	Account Name	Debit	Credit
8/21/2019	Office Supplies & Software	100	
	Accounts Payable		100

In our example, the debit to **Office Supplies & Software** increases the total expenses on the income statement by $100. In addition, the credit to A/P increases total liabilities by $100 on the balance sheet report. In order to stay on top of your bills, it's a good idea to enter them as soon as you receive them. Be sure to enter a due date, so that QuickBooks can alert you when a bill is becoming due. Next, we will show you how to pay bills.

Paying bills in QuickBooks Online

After you enter a bill in QuickBooks, you will need to pay it before the due date. Paying bills in QuickBooks will ensure the A/P balance is always up to date and will allow you to run reports, and to see which bills have been paid or need to be paid.

Follow these steps to pay bills in QuickBooks Online:

1. Navigate to the Quick Create menu and select **Pay Bills** listed in the **Vendors** column, as indicated in the following screenshot:

2. Complete the key fields in the **Pay Bills** form, as indicated in the following screenshot:

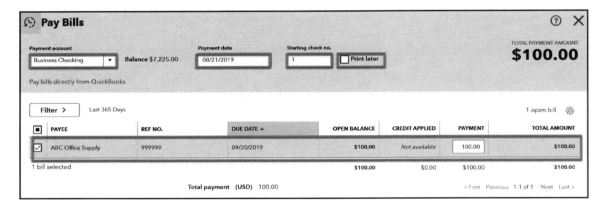

The following is a brief description of the fields in the **Pay Bills** form:

- **Payment account**: Select the bank or credit card account from which you want to deduct this bill payment.
- **Payment date**: Select the date on which you will pay for this bill. If writing a check, this will be the check date.
- **Starting check no.**: If you are writing a check, make sure the check number is the next available number.
- **Print later**: Put a check in this box if you don't plan to print the check now, but will print it later on.
- **PAYEE**: This field will include a list of the payees with open bills. To select a bill for payment, put a checkmark in the box to the left of the **PAYEE** field.

- **REF NO.:** This field will include the invoice number (or bill number) that was entered when the bill was saved in QuickBooks.
- **DUE DATE**: This field will automatically populate with the due date that was entered when the bill was saved in QuickBooks.
- **OPEN BALANCE**: This field will automatically populate with the unpaid amount of the bill.
- **CREDIT APPLIED**: If you have open credits for a vendor, you will see them listed in this column.
- **PAYMENT**: Enter the amount you would like to pay in this field. You can pay the bill in full, or make a partial payment. If you make a partial payment, QuickBooks will keep the remaining balance due on file for you to pay in the future.
- **TOTAL AMOUNT**: This column is automatically calculated for you. It should equal the amount you entered in the **PAYMENT** field.

When you pay a bill in QuickBooks, it only has an impact on the balance sheet report. The A/P balance goes down because you no longer owe your vendor for the bill, and the business checking account goes down because a payment has been made. If you paid the bill with a credit card, the credit card balance goes up, which increases liabilities.

The following screenshot shows the journal entry recorded for the preceding bill:

Date	Account Name	Debit	Credit
8/21/2019	Accounts Payable	100	
	Business Checking		100

In our example, the debit to A/P decreases total liabilities on the balance sheet report by $100. In addition, the credit to the business checking account decreases total assets on the balance sheet report by **$100**. Paying bills in QuickBooks will give you access to detailed information about your expenses. You can run reports to show you how much you are spending, which vendors you purchase from, and how often. These reports will help you to control what you are spending your money on, which allows you to properly manage your expenses. Creating recurring expenses in QuickBooks can save you a lot of time. We will cover how to manage recurring expenses next.

Managing recurring expenses

Most businesses purchase goods and services from the same vendors. For example, rent and utilities are examples of recurring expenses that are generally paid monthly. Instead of creating these expenses from scratch each month, you can create a recurring expense, which is a template you can save with the vendor, amount, account, and other pertinent information.

When you are ready to pay a recurring expense, you can schedule the expense to automatically record on a certain day. You can manually generate the expense when you need to pay it or have QuickBooks send you an alert when it's time to make a payment. Using recurring expense templates will save you time, and will reduce the amount of manual data entry required.

Follow these steps to create a recurring expense in QuickBooks:

1. Navigate to the gear icon and select **Recurring Transactions** from the **Lists** column, as indicated in the following screenshot:

2. Select the transaction type from the drop-down menu, as indicated in the following screenshot:

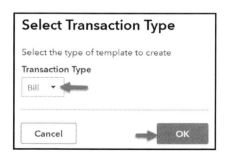

3. The **Recurring Transactions** template will be displayed, as indicated in the following screenshot:

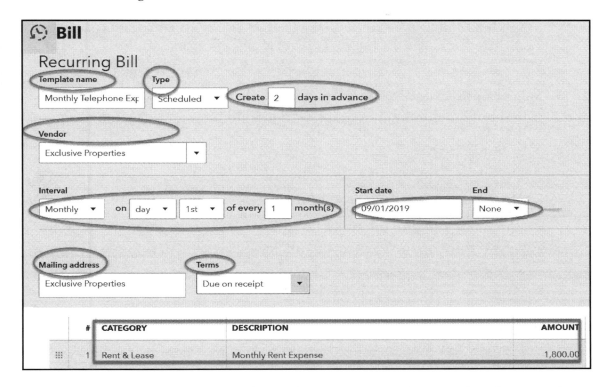

The following is a brief description of the information required to complete the **Recurring Transactions** template:

- **Template name**: This field should include the type of expense or the payee's name.
- **Type**: From the drop-down menu, you can select **Scheduled**, **Reminder**, or **Unscheduled**.
- **Number of days**: QuickBooks will create the transaction in advance of the due date.
- **Vendor**: Select the payee from the drop-down menu. If you have not added vendors to QuickBooks, you can add a new vendor by selecting **Add new** in the drop-down field.
- **Interval**: This field refers to how often you would like to create this recurring transaction. The options are **Daily**, **Weekly**, **Monthly**, or **Yearly**.

- **Start date/End**: Select the date on which you would like to start using the recurring transaction and, if applicable, you can select an end date, or select **None**.
- **Mailing address**: If you plan to mail your payment, you need to add a mailing address to this field. However, if the payment is automatically deducted from your business checking account or made using a credit card, you can leave this field blank.
- **Terms**: Include the payment terms for the vendor in this field.
- **CATEGORY**: From the drop-down menu, select the account that accurately describes the type of purchase made.
- **DESCRIPTION**: Include a brief description of the expense in this field.
- **AMOUNT**: Enter the amount of the expense in this field.

4. After saving the template, the **Recurring Transactions** template list will be displayed, as indicated in the following screenshot:

TEMPLATE NAME	TYPE	TXN TYPE	INTERVAL ▲	PREVI	NEXT DATE	CUSTOMER/VENDOR	AMOUNT
Monthly Telephone Expense	Scheduled	Bill	Every Month		09/01/20…	Exclusive Properties	1,800.00

In addition to creating recurring transactions such as bills and checks to pay expenses, you can also create the following types of recurring transactions:

- **Credit card credit**: Credit card credit is money that was refunded to you from a previous credit card charge. This could also be a cashback rebate given to you by your credit card merchant for meeting a certain spending threshold.
- **Credit memo**: A credit memo is issued to customers for a product they have returned or for services that were not provided.
- **Deposit**: A deposit is money received from customers, which is then deposited into your bank account. If you have customers who pay via wire transfer or **Automated Clearing House (ACH)** bank transfer on a periodic basis, you could set these deposits up as recurring.
- **Estimate**: An estimate is a bid or quote, created to provide customers with an approximate cost of your products or services.
- **Invoice**: An invoice is a sales form, used to record the sale of products or services provided on credit.

- **Journal entry**: A journal entry form is used to make adjustments to the financial statements before closing the books.
- **Purchase order**: A **purchase order (PO)** is used to place an order for products with a vendor supplier.
- **Refund**: A product returned by you or your customer will result in a refund of the payment that was made for the returned goods or unfulfilled services.
- **Sales receipt**: A sales receipt is used to record sales whereby payment is made immediately by the customer (for example, businesses such as clothing stores or restaurants).
- **Transfer**: A transfer is used to move money between bank accounts, such as business checking and savings accounts.
- **Vendor credit**: A vendor credit is a refund issued to you by a vendor supplier for a product you have returned or for services that were not performed.

If you need to pay a bill that was unexpected or past due, you don't need to enter it as a bill, and then pay it. Instead, you can go directly to the check register and write a check. We will cover writing checks in the next section.

Writing checks

So far, we have discussed how to pay expenses by entering them as bills and paying them at a later date, and how to set up recurring expenses. A third way you can record expenses for your business is by writing checks. The benefit of writing checks directly in QuickBooks is that you don't have to waste time manually writing a check. Instead, you can create checks and print them directly from QuickBooks.

Follow these steps for writing checks in QuickBooks Online:

1. Navigate to the Quick Create menu and select **Check** listed in the **Vendors** column, as indicated in the following screenshot:

2. The following screenshot shows the fields of information to be completed in the **Check** form:

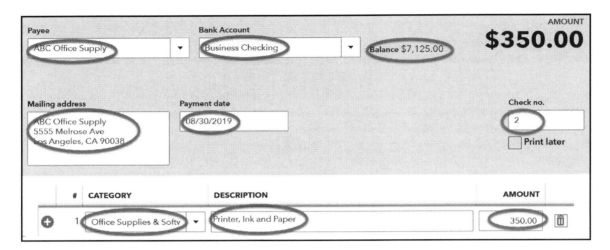

The following is a brief description of the information in the preceding **Check** form:

- **Payee**: From the drop-down menu, select the vendor to whom you are making a payment. If you have not added vendors, you can do so by selecting **Add new** from the drop-down menu.
- **Bank Account**: This field will automatically populate with your business checking account. However, if you have more than one checking account, be sure to select the correct account from the drop-down menu.
- **Balance**: Based on the bank account selected, you will see the current balance (per QuickBooks) of the business checking account you have selected.
- **Mailing address**: This field will automatically populate with the information on file for the payee.
- **Payment date**: This date should reflect the check date.
- **Check no.**: The check number will automatically populate with the next available check number.

You can also use the **Write Checks** form to record expenses paid with a debit card. Instead of entering a check number in the **Check no.** field, you would use **DB** or **Debit,** indicating the expense was paid with a debit card.

- **CATEGORY**: Select the category (account) that best describes the items purchased.
- **DESCRIPTION**: Enter a detailed description of the items purchased.
- **AMOUNT**: Enter the amount of the purchase.

When entering a check into QuickBooks, it can have an impact on accounts that appear on both the balance sheet and the profit and loss (income statement). The balance sheet will always be affected because the bank account is included in the assets section of the balance sheet. However, the profit and loss will only be affected if you purchase an expense. Otherwise, if you purchase the product for resale (inventory), it will only have an impact on the balance sheet.

The following screenshot shows the journal entry recorded for the preceding **Check** form:

Date	Account Name	Debit	Credit
8/30/2019	Office Supplies & Software	350	
	Business Checking		350

In our example, **Office Supplies & Software** increased by $350, which increases expenses on the profit and loss (income statement). The business checking account decreased by $350, which means assets have gone down on the balance sheet report.

After entering a check, you can choose to print the check immediately, or wait and print a batch of checks later on. In the next section, we will show you how to print checks.

Printing checks

In order to print checks, you must purchase a check stock that is compatible with QuickBooks Online. You can order checks from a variety of places, such as your financial institution, or directly from Intuit. Visit the `Intuit Checks and Supplies` website to learn more.

Follow these steps to print checks:

1. Navigate to the Quick Create menu and select **Print Checks** listed in the **Vendors** column, as indicated in the following screenshot:

2. Follow these steps to ensure your printer is set up properly:

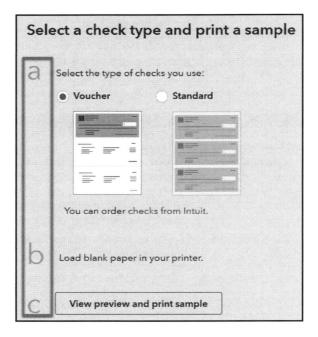

The following is a brief description of the steps outlined previously:

- **Select the type of checks you use**: There are two types of checks (**Voucher** and **Standard**). The **Voucher** check includes one check per page, and two printed vouchers (one for you and one for the payee). The **Standard** check has three checks per page, and no voucher.
- **Load blank paper in your printer**: Before loading real check stock, run a test using blank paper.
- **View preview and print sample**: You can preview a sample check to see whether it is aligned properly. If not, follow the onscreen instructions to fix any issues before using real check stock.

As discussed, printing checks directly from QuickBooks will save you time when you reconcile your bank account. Since expenses paid with a check are automatically recorded in QuickBooks when you save the check, you won't have to worry about manually entering them later on.

Summary

As stated at the beginning of this chapter, we have shown you how to enter and pay your bills, how to manage recurring expenses, how to write checks, and how to print checks. As a result, you will be able to stay on top of your cash outflow. In the next chapter, we will show you how to reduce or eliminate manually entering bank and credit card transactions by downloading transactions automatically into QuickBooks.

8
Managing Downloaded Bank and Credit Card Transactions

In Chapter 4, *Customizing QuickBooks for your Business*, we showed you how to connect bank and credit card accounts to **QuickBooks Online** (**QBO**), to reduce the amount of time you spend manually entering data. In this chapter, we will show you how to manage bank and credit card transactions that have been downloaded to QuickBooks. When bank and credit card transactions are downloaded, they are organized in the banking center. Before these transactions can be recorded in QuickBooks, you must review them, with respect to matching them with transactions that have already been entered into QuickBooks, adding payee or category information, and providing any additional details, to help identify each transaction. We will also show you how bank rules can help to reduce the number of transactions requiring manual review. Last, but not least, we will show you how to reconcile your accounts. Reconciling is the process of making sure your QuickBooks data matches the monthly statements provided by your financial institution. By reconciling often, you can catch errors made by the bank or credit card company, and catch fraudulent transactions a lot sooner.

In this chapter, we will cover the following topics:

- Overview of the banking center
- Matching transactions
- Editing banking transactions
- Creating and using bank rules
- Reconciling accounts

We will start by giving you an overview of the banking center, which is where you will find downloaded bank and credit card transactions.

Overview of the banking center

The banking center is where you can manage bank and credit card transactions that have been downloaded into QuickBooks from your financial institution. At the very top of the page, you will see tiles that represent bank and credit card accounts you have added to QuickBooks. On each tile, you will find the name of the account, the current balance (per your financial institution), the current balance (per QuickBooks), and the number of transactions that require review before they can be recorded in the QuickBooks check register.

Follow these steps to navigate to the banking center:

1. Click on the **Banking** tab, located on the left menu bar, as indicated in the following screenshot:

2. The banking center will be displayed, as indicated in the following screenshot:

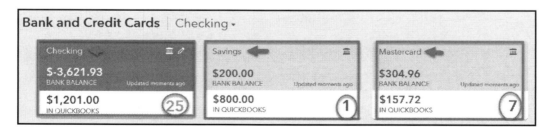

The following is a brief description of the information you will find in the banking center:

- **Bank account**: At the very top of each tile, you will find the name of the account (for example, **Checking**, **Savings**, **Mastercard**).
- **BANK BALANCE**: The balance of the account per your financial institution will be displayed below the bank account name.

- **BALANCE IN QUICKBOOKS:** The balance of the account per QuickBooks will be displayed right below the bank balance.
- **Transactions for review:** Transactions that have been downloaded from your financial institution and are pending review will be indicated in the lower right-hand corner of each tile.

 If the bank balance and the balance in QuickBooks match, this means all downloaded transactions have been reviewed. As a result, you will not see a number in the lower right-hand corner of the tile.

If you imported your transactions into QuickBooks from a CSV file instead of connecting your bank and credit card accounts to QuickBooks, you will only see a QuickBooks balance (not a bank balance) for each account. I recommend reviewing transactions on a daily or weekly basis so that you don't get too far behind.

Next, we will show you how QuickBooks can save you time by matching transactions that you have already entered into QuickBooks.

Matching transactions

One of the benefits of having transactions automatically download into QuickBooks from your financial institution is that the software will check to see if the transaction was previously recorded, or if there is a related transaction.

In the following screenshot, QuickBooks has attempted to match three transactions:

1 record found Deposit 08/05/2019 $868.15	$868.15	➡ **Match**
1 record found Check 75 08/05/2019 $228.7 Hicks Hardware	$228.75	**Match**
1 record found Bill Payment 6 08/04/2019 $114.09	$114.09	**Match**

The following is a brief explanation of the preceding three transactions:

- **Deposit for $868.15**: QuickBooks has found a deposit in the file for **$868.15** (dated **08/05/19**), which matches a deposit the bank has downloaded to the banking center for **$868.15**. If these transactions are one and the same, you would simply click **Match** in the far-right column.
- **Check for $228.75**: QuickBooks has identified **Check#75** for **$228.75**, which matches a withdrawal downloaded from the bank for the same amount (**$228.75**). If these transactions are one and the same, you would simply click **Match** in the far-right column.
- **Bill Payment for $114.09**: QuickBooks has found a bill payment for **$114.09**, which matches a withdrawal downloaded from the bank for the same amount (**$114.09**). If these transactions are one and the same, you would simply click **Match** in the far-right column.

When you select **Match**, these items will move from the **For Review** tab to the **Reviewed** tab in the banking center. These items will also be marked as cleared in QuickBooks, which will be important when we get ready to reconcile these accounts later on. If QuickBooks has not found the right match, you can replace it with the correct match.

To change the match recommended by QuickBooks, click on the transaction, and then click on the **Find other records** button, as indicated in the following screenshot:

In addition to matching transactions, you will need to provide additional information, such as payee and category (account), before the transaction can be recorded in QuickBooks. In the next section, we will cover how to edit banking transactions.

Editing banking transactions

When you first start adding banking transactions to QuickBooks, you will need to review each transaction to ensure it has a proper payee (vendor) and account category assigned to it. As you begin to repeat transactions, QuickBooks will remember how a transaction was recorded previously, and it will automatically assign the payee (vendor) and account category for you.

Follow these steps to edit banking transactions in the banking center:

1. From the left menu bar, select **Banking**, as indicated in the following screenshot:

2. Click on the **For Review** tab, as indicated in the following screenshot:

3. Click anywhere within the transaction you want to edit, as indicated in the following screenshot:

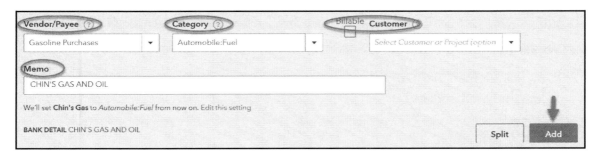

You will find the following information in the edit banking transaction window:

- **Vendor/Payee**: For withdrawals, select the payee (vendor) or customer from the drop-down menu. If it is a new payee (vendor) or customer, you can click **Add new** from the drop-down menu, and add them here.

- **Category**: From the drop-down menu, select the category (account) that best describes the transaction you are recording (that is, Fuel; Office Supplies).
- **Billable and Customer**: If recording an expense you need to bill to a customer, tick the **Billable** checkbox, then select the customer from the drop-down menu so that this transaction is earmarked as a billable expense.
- **Memo**: The bank details will generally appear in this field. This could be the name of the merchant.
- **Add**: Once all fields are complete, click on the **Add** button to add this transaction to the check or credit card register in QuickBooks.

As discussed, QuickBooks will automatically recall the vendor (payee) and category (account) that was previously used. However, the best way to ensure this information is accurate is to create bank rules. We will discuss how to create and use bank rules in the next section.

Understanding bank rules

Bank rules are a list of conditions that must be met in order for QuickBooks to automatically assign a payee, account (category), class, and a location to download banking transactions. Bank rules will apply only to bank or credit card transactions in the **For Review** tab of the banking center. Since most businesses have the same transactions that take place month after month, using bank rules can save you the time you would have spent reviewing transactions in the banking center, before they are recorded in QuickBooks.

Follow these steps to create a bank rule:

1. Click on the **Banking** tab, located on the left menu bar, as indicated in the following screenshot:

2. Click on the **Rules** tab, as indicated in the following screenshot:

3. Click on the **New rule** button, as indicated in the following screenshot:

4. The following screen will be displayed:

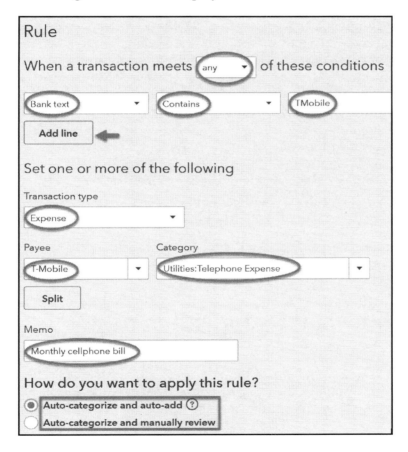

The following is a brief explanation of the fields to complete for a new bank rule:

- **Application of conditions**: The first field allows you to determine if a transaction must meet **any** condition or **all** conditions. In our example, we have selected **any**.
- **Conditions:** You can create several conditions based on the **Bank text**, **Description**, or **Amount**. In our example, we have selected **Bank text**.
- **Contains**, **Doesn't contain**, **Is exactly**: In the next field, you can select whether the transaction contains, doesn't contain, or is exactly the information that you enter into the next field.
- **Text box**: This field will contain text that will appear either in the bank text or description field when the transaction is downloaded into QuickBooks. If you selected the amount as part of your criteria, then you will enter an amount in this field. In our text box, we have put **T-Mobile**, which is the name of the payee.
- You can click the **Add line** button to add multiple conditions. Based on the conditions you have set, QuickBooks will automatically code the transaction, using the information below the **Set one or more of the following** heading.
- **Transaction type**: From the drop-down menu, select the type of transaction for which you are creating this rule. In our example, this is an **Expense**.
- **Payee**: From the drop-down menu, select the payee for this rule. In our example, the payee is **T-Mobile**.
- **Category**: From the drop-down menu, select the category (account) that best describes the purchase. In our example, we have selected **Telephone Expense**.
- **Split**: If the transaction should be split between two or more accounts (categories), you can click this **Split** button, and indicate the accounts that should be used.
- **Memo**: This field is optional, but can be used to provide additional details about the transaction. In our example, we have used **Monthly cellphone bill**.

How do you want to apply this rule?

In this section, there are two options:

- **Auto-categorize and auto-add**: By selecting this option, QuickBooks will automatically assign the category (account) based on your selections above, and will automatically record the transaction in QuickBooks, without you reviewing it first.

- **Auto-categorize and manually review**: By selecting this option, QuickBooks will automatically assign the category (account) based on your selections above, and will leave the transaction in the **For Review** tab, so that you can manually review it and add it to QuickBooks.

> Set all bank rules to **Auto-categorize and manually review** first. After you have reviewed the transactions for the first couple of months and are comfortable they are being categorized correctly, you can always change the bank rules to **Auto-categorize and auto-add** later on.

If set up properly, bank rules can automatically categorize and record 80% or more of your bank and credit card transactions. If you have a lot of transactions coming through, this will save you hours of time, which you can spend on other aspects of your business. Start with one bank rule to see how it works, and then add more as you get comfortable with using them. Using bank rules will also help to expedite the reconciliation of bank and credit card accounts. We will discuss this in more detail next.

Reconciling accounts

Reconciling is the process of making sure your QuickBooks records agree with your bank and credit card statements. At a minimum, reconciling should take place on a monthly basis, if not more often. One of the benefits of using cloud-based accounting software such as QBO is that your banking information is downloaded on a daily basis. This means that you could reconcile as often as daily, or even weekly. There is no need to wait until the bank statement arrives at the end of the month to reconcile your accounts.

Follow these steps to reconcile a bank or credit card account:

1. From the gear icon, select **Reconcile**, as indicated in the following screenshot:

2. The start reconciliation window will be displayed, as indicated in the following screenshot:

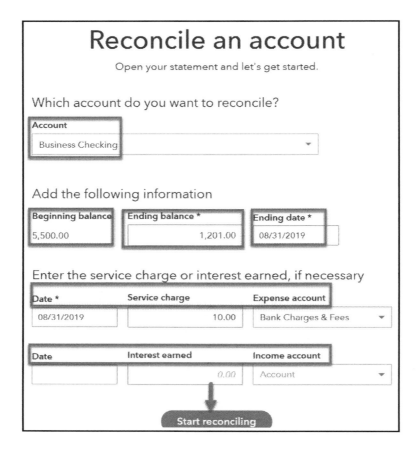

The fields that need to be completed in the reconciliation window previously shown are as follows:

- **Account**: From the drop-down menu, select the bank or credit card account you want to reconcile.
- **Beginning balance**: The **Beginning balance** field will automatically populate with the ending balance of the previous month. If you have never reconciled the account before, the balance in this field will be the opening balance entered when you created the account in QuickBooks.

- **Ending balance**: Enter the ending balance of the bank or credit card statement you are reconciling.

- **Ending date**: Enter the ending date on the bank or credit card statement you are reconciling. In general, it will be the last day of the month (for example, **08/31/2019**).

- **Service charge**: If the bank charges a service charge, enter that information in this field, along with the ending date of the statement. These charges should be categorized into a bank service charges and fees account.

- **Interest earned**: If you have earned interest, you will enter this information, along with the ending date of the statement. Interest earned should be categorized into an **Interest Income** account.

Click the **Start reconciling** button once all of these fields have been completed.

In the next screen, the following information will be displayed.

The following is a snapshot of the header information when reconciling accounts:

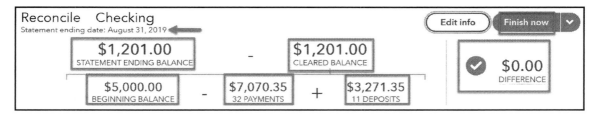

A brief description of the information found in the header window is as follows:

- **STATEMENT ENDING BALANCE**: This field will automatically populate with the statement ending balance entered in the preceding start reconciliation screen.

- **CLEARED BALANCE**: This field will summarize all the transactions that have cleared on your bank or credit card statement.

- **BEGINNING BALANCE**: This field will automatically populate from the prior month's reconciliation. If you have not reconciled this account previously, it will display the beginning balance entered when the account was created in QuickBooks.

- **PAYMENTS/WITHDRAWALS**: This field will summarize all of the payments/withdrawals that have cleared on your bank or credit card statement.
- **DEPOSITS**: This field will summarize all of the deposits that have cleared on your bank or credit card statement.
- **DIFFERENCE**: The difference between the statement ending balance and the cleared balance will appear in this field. The goal is to reach a difference of zero. Zero indicates all items that have cleared your bank or credit card statement have been recorded in QuickBooks.
- **Finish now**: After your difference equals zero, you can click the **Finish now** button to generate the bank reconciliation reports.

Do not click the **Finish now** button if you don't have a difference of zero. Instead, click the drop-down arrow next to **Finish now**, and select **Finish later**. You can always come back, and resume the reconciliation where you left off.

The following is a snapshot of the detailed bank and credit card information that appears after the header information:

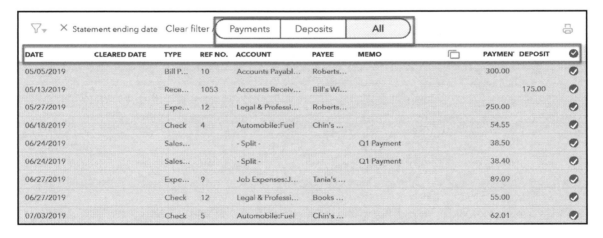

DATE	CLEARED DATE	TYPE	REF NO.	ACCOUNT	PAYEE	MEMO		PAYMEN'	DEPOSIT	
05/05/2019		Bill P...	10	Accounts Payabl...	Roberts...			300.00		
05/13/2019		Rece...	1053	Accounts Receiv...	Bill's Wi...				175.00	
05/27/2019		Expe...	12	Legal & Professi...	Roberts...			250.00		
06/18/2019		Check	4	Automobile:Fuel	Chin's ...			54.55		
06/24/2019		Sales...		- Split -		Q1 Payment		38.50		
06/24/2019		Sales...		- Split -		Q1 Payment		38.40		
06/27/2019		Expe...	9	Job Expenses:J...	Tania's ...			89.09		
06/27/2019		Check	12	Legal & Professi...	Books ...			55.00		
07/03/2019		Check	5	Automobile:Fuel	Chin's ...			62.01		

The following is a brief explanation of the detailed reconciliation window, shown in the preceding screenshot:

- **Transaction type**: At the top of the screen, there are three tabs: **Payments**, **Deposits**, and **All**. You can click on one of the first two tabs to filter on a specific transaction type, or you can select **All**.
- **Transaction details**: The date, transaction type, reference number, category (account), payee memo, and amount of each transaction that has been recorded in QuickBooks is listed in the details section.

If a transaction appears on your bank or credit card account, you need to put a checkmark in the radio button (located in the far right column) to mark it as cleared in QuickBooks. Each time you mark a transaction as cleared, it will be included in the cleared balance in the header section shown previously. As discussed, after marking all items that have cleared your bank or credit card statement, you should have a difference of zero. If you do not, you are either missing a transaction in QuickBooks or you may have marked a transaction as cleared that does not appear on your statement.

If you are having trouble reconciling to a difference of zero, compare the deposit total in the header window to the deposit total on your bank statement. If it matches, then you know there is an issue with withdrawals. If it doesn't match, then you know there is an issue with deposits. Do the same comparison on the withdrawal side. You could be out of balance with both, or with just one transaction type.

After successfully reconciling accounts, be sure to save the summary and detailed bank reconciliation reports. Bank reconciliation reports are one of several reports that auditors will request.

As discussed, reconciling your accounts will help to ensure you haven't accidentally omitted recording transactions. Plus, it will help you to ensure that your books agree with your financial institution's records. It's important to reconcile all of your bank and credit card accounts on a monthly basis (or more frequently, if possible), in order to catch errors made by the bank or to identify fraudulent transactions.

Summary

In this chapter, we have discussed how to manage downloaded bank and credit card transactions. You have learned how to match downloaded transactions with transactions previously recorded in QuickBooks. You now know how to make changes to transactions so that the correct payee and category (account) is recorded. You have also learned how to create bank rules in order to reduce the number of transactions you need to review in the banking center, which will save you time. Finally, you know the importance of reconciling bank and credit card accounts on a frequent basis, to ensure your records are in sync with your financial institution.

We have met our goal of giving you the knowledge to successfully manage your downloaded bank and credit card transactions. Having this knowledge will help you to save the time you would have normally spent manually entering bank and credit card transactions into QuickBooks.

It will also help you to become familiar with how much money you are spending, as well as what you are spending it on. Remember, having the ability to control your expenses will help to improve your bottom line.

In the next chapter, we will show you how to generate reports in QuickBooks. There are a number of preset reports in QuickBooks, which means you never have to create a report from scratch. You will learn how to customize existing reports and export them to Excel/PDF or send them as attachments via email.

Report Center Overview 9

Now that you know how to enter income and expenses into QuickBooks, it's time to learn how to generate reports to gain insight into the overall health of your business. In this chapter, we will show you how to navigate the report center, give you an overview of the reports available, show you how to customize reports to meet your business needs, and how to share those reports with your accountant and business stakeholders.

Understanding how to run reports will help you to gain insight into all aspects of your business. Having access to your income, expenses, and other key performance indicators will help you to make good business decisions.

The following topics will be covered in this chapter:

- Navigating the report center
- Reports available in the report center
- Customizing reports
- Exporting reports
- Sending reports via email

Navigating the report center

The report center includes several pre-built reports that will give you both a summary and detailed information about various aspects of your business. It is organized into three main sections: standard reports, custom reports, and management reports. The majority of the reports are located in the standard reports section.

Standard reports are categorized into the following nine reporting groups:

- **Favorites**: You can mark your most frequently used reports as a favorite and they will be listed in the favorites group.
- **Business overview**: The business overview group includes reports that provide insight into the overall health of your business. You will find both a detailed and summarized overview of profit and loss, the balance sheet, and a statement of cash flow reports in this group.
- **Who owes you**: Money owed to you by your customers is also known as accounts receivable (A/R). In this group, you will find reports to help you to stay on top of your A/R balances. The A/R aging detail and summary, open invoices, and collections reports can be found in this group.
- **Sales and customers**: The sales and customer group includes detailed and summary reports that will give you insight into who your top customers are and what products and services they are buying. Income by customer, products and services list, and sales by customer are just a few of the reports you will find in this group.
- **What you owe**: Money you owe to others is also known as accounts payable (A/P). In this group, you will find reports to help you to stay on top of your A/P balances. A/P aging, bill payment list, and unpaid bills are just a few of the reports you will find in this group.
- **Expenses and vendors**: The expenses and vendors group includes reports that will give you insight into who and what you are spending your money on. Some examples of reports you will find in this group are check detail, expenses by vendor, and open purchase orders.
- **Employees**: If you have added employees to QuickBooks, this group includes reports that will provide you with employee information. Employee contact list and time activities are a couple of reports that you will find in this group. If you manage payroll in QuickBooks, head over to the payroll reports group for more detailed payroll reports.
- **For my accountant**: Reports that assist your accountant in preparing your taxes can be found in the **For my accountant** reports group. You will find profit and loss, balance sheet reports, and a list of the chart of accounts along with many other reports in this group.
- **Payroll**: If you have the payroll feature turned on, you will have access to several detailed and summary payroll reports by employee, location, and class.

Custom reports will include any report you have made customizations to and saved. We will discuss how to customize reports later on.

Management reports are the third group of reports, and they include professional report packages that you can download and customize with items such as a cover page and a table of contents. These reports can be used when presenting financial statements to a board of directors or a financial institution when seeking financing. The number of reports you can access depends on your **QuickBooks Online (QBO)** subscription level. In the next section, we will cover the reports included in each QBO subscription.

Reports available in the Report Center

In Chapter 1, *Getting Started with QuickBooks Online*, we discussed the four subscription levels you can purchase for QBO: Simple Start, Essentials, Plus, and Advanced. Depending on the subscription level you have purchased, you could have access to anywhere between 20 and 100 or more reports. Simple Start includes more than 20 reports, Essentials includes more than 40 reports, Plus includes more than 65 reports, and Advanced includes more than 100 reports.

The following is a breakdown of some of the reports you will find in each QBO subscription.

QBO Simple Start includes more than 20 reports, some of which are listed as follows:

Profit & Loss	Sales by Customer
Balance Sheet	Sales by Product/Services
Statement of Cash Flows	Transaction List by Vendor
Customer Balance Summary	Check Detail
A/R Aging Summary	Payroll Reports (if payroll is on)
Taxable Sales	Customized Reports
Transaction List by Date	Product/Service List
Reconciliation Reports	Deposit Detail

In addition to the reports included in Simple Start, QBO Essentials includes 40 plus reports, including the following:

A/P Aging	**Profit & Loss Detail**
Bill Payment List	**Sales by Customer Detail**
Company Snapshot	**Terms Listing**
Customer Balance Detail	**Trial Balance**
Expenses by Vendor	**Unbilled Charges**
General Ledger	**Unpaid Bills**
Income by Customer Summary	**Vendor Balance**

In addition to the reports included in Simple Start and Essentials, QBO Plus has more than 65 plus reports, including the following:

Budget Overview	**Purchases by Product/Service**
Buget vs. Actuals	**Purchases by Location/Class**
Class Listing	**Sales by Location or Class**
Profit & Loss by Class	**Time Activities by Customer**
Profit & Loss by Location	**Time Activities by Employee**
Open Purchase Orders	**Transaction Detail by Account**

In addition to the reports included in Simple Start, Essentials, and Plus, QBO Advanced has more than 100 reports. It also includes a smart reporting tool called Fathom. Smart reporting takes the data from your QuickBooks file and puts it into easy-to-understand reports that will give you insight into profitability, cash flow, and other key performance indicators.

In the next section, we will show you how to customize reports to meet your business requirements.

Customizing reports

As discussed, you don't have to create a report from scratch in QuickBooks Online. However, you can customize an existing report to get the data that you need. You can save any changes you make to a report so you don't have to recreate it each time.

The following are the steps to customize a report:

1. Click on **Reports** on the left menu bar to navigate to the report center, as indicated here:

2. Select the report as indicated:

3. Click the **Customize** button located in the upper-right corner:

4. The following customization window will be displayed:

As indicated in the preceding screenshot, there are four primary areas you can customize:

- **General**
- **Rows/Columns**
- **Filter**
- **Header/Footer**

We will cover these areas in the following sections.

General report customizations

In general report customizations, you can select **Report period**, **Accounting method**, and how you would like numbers formatted on any report:

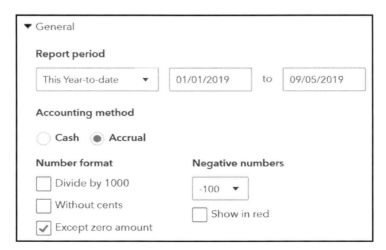

The following is a brief explanation of what's included in general customizations:

- **Report period**: Select the period you would like to see in the report. You can do this by selecting the preset time frames from the drop-down menu or entering the dates directly in the fields.
- **Accounting method**: You can select the accounting method you would like to see the report in (**Cash** or **Accrual**). Reports will automatically default to the accounting method chosen when you set up your QuickBooks account. However, you can change this directly on the report. To change the default accounting method, go to **Company preferences** and select the **Accounting** tab to make this change.
- **Number format**: You can format numbers by dividing them by 1,000, removing the cents, and not showing anything with a zero amount.
- **Negative numbers**: From the drop-down menu, you can choose to show negative numbers in one of three ways. The negative sign can be in front of the number or behind the number, or the negative numbers can be in parentheses, for example, **-100, 100-**, or **(100)**.

Rows/Columns customization

Rows/Columns customization includes formatting columns, comparing the current data to a previous period, and comparing the number of columns and rows to the grand total on the report:

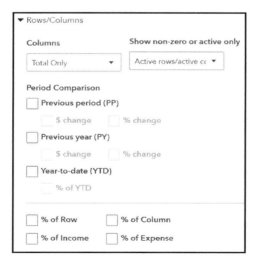

The following is a brief explanation of what's included in **Rows/Columns** customizations:

- **Columns**: Displays column information by showing totals only, by period (days, weeks, month), or by customers, vendors, or employees.
- **Show non-zero or active only**: Select to only show non-zero data or all active data (with and without zeros).
- **Period Comparison**: This allows you to see how the current period compares to a previous period, year, or year-to-date. This change can be shown in both a percentage format, dollar amount, or both.
- **% of Row or % of Column**: Select **% of Row** or **% of Column** to see the percentage of each item listed on the report compared to other items on the same row or column of the report.
- **% of Income or % of Expense**: Select **% of Income** and the program will calculate what percent of each item listed on the report makes up the total income reported. A similar calculation is done when you select **% of Expense** but using the total expenses reported.

Filters

To customize reports for specific data, you can filter reports by **Distribution Account**, **Customer**, **Vendor**, **Employee**, and **Product/Service**. To filter a report, put a checkmark in the box to the left of the filter and make your selection from the drop-down menu, as follows:

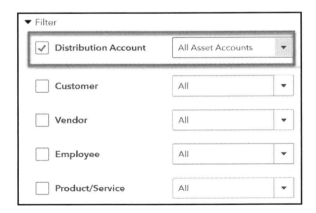

Next, let's talk a bit about the headers and footers.

Header/footer

You can also customize the header and footer information that appears on reports. This can be useful if you have filtered a report in such a way that the current title is no longer applicable.

To customize the header, you can add a logo, update/change the name of the company that appears on the report, and change the title of the report. You can also choose to have the dates displayed on the report or remove them.

The following is a screenshot of the **Header** information that can be customized on reports:

To customize the footer, you can choose whether or not to display the date when the report was prepared, the time the report was prepared, and the report basis.

The following is a snapshot of the **Footer** information that can be customized on reports:

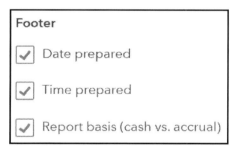

Now that you know how to customize reports to fit your business needs, you are ready to learn how to share reports. You can export reports to Excel, PDF, a printer, or email them directly from QuickBooks. Let's talk about how to export reports in the next section.

Exporting reports

You have several options to choose from when it comes to exporting your QuickBooks data. Like most programs, you can print a hard copy of any report. If you need to manipulate the data or add additional information, exporting the data to Excel might be a good option. If you need to share your data with your accountant, a board member, or anyone who does not have access to QuickBooks, you can save any report as a PDF document and email the report. Finally, you can email a report directly from QuickBooks. When you select the email option, you can send it to multiple people and copy anyone that you need to. When sending a report via email, the report will be attached as a PDF document.

In this section, we will cover how to export reports to Excel and PDF. In the next section, we will show you the step-by-step process of emailing reports directly from QuickBooks.

When you run a report in QuickBooks, the export data menu will automatically display in the upper right-hand as indicated here:

The following is a brief explanation of each icon:

- **Envelope**: Click on the icon that resembles an envelope if you want to email a report directly from QuickBooks.
- **Printer**: The icon that resembles a printer is used if you would like to print a hard copy of a report.
- **Paper**: The icon that resembles a sheet of paper with an arrow going through it is used to export reports to Excel or PDF. We will discuss how this works next.

Exporting reports to Excel

As discussed in the previous section, if you need the ability to manipulate the data on a report or add additional columns and rows, you can export reports to Excel.

Follow these steps to export a report to Excel:

1. Navigate to the reports center by clicking on **Reports** on the left menu bar, as follows:

2. Select the reporting group that includes the report you wish to run, as follows:

3. Choose the report you wish to run, as follows:

4. The report will be displayed on your screen:

5. Click on the icon that resembles a sheet of paper with an arrow going through it, as shown in the following:

6. Choose **Export to Excel**, as follows:

7. Your report should display in Excel, as follows:

Photos By Design, LLC		
Profit and Loss		
January 1 - September 9, 2019		
		Total
Income		
Photography Services		275.00
Sales		1,800.00
Total Income	$	2,075.00
Gross Profit	$	2,075.00
Expenses		
Office Supplies & Software		450.00
Rent & Lease		1,800.00
Total Expenses	$	2,250.00
Net Operating Income	-$	175.00
Net Income	-$	175.00

At this point, you can save the report to your computer and make any necessary changes.

If the report does not immediately display on your screen, look at the very bottom of the screen and there should be an Excel icon. Click on it to display the report in Excel.

If you need to send reports to anyone outside of the company, I recommend you export the reports to PDF instead of Excel. Let's discuss how to export reports to PDF.

Exporting reports to PDF

If you need to share reports with your accountant, members on your board of directors, or a financial institution, exporting the reports to a PDF file is a great option. The first five steps in exporting reports to PDF are identical to the first five steps covered in exporting reports to Excel (in the previous section). Once you have completed the first five steps, perform the following steps to export reports to PDF.

Follow these steps to export reports in a PDF format:

1. Click on **Export to PDF** as indicated here:

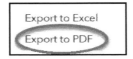

2. The PDF report will be displayed on your screen, as indicated here:

You can save the report to your computer by clicking on the arrow pointing down in the upper right-hand corner or you can print a hard copy of the report by clicking on the print button next to the arrow, as shown in the preceding screenshot.

That wraps up three of the four primary ways you can export your data out of QuickBooks. In the next section, we will cover how to send reports via email directly from QuickBooks.

Sending reports via email

Sending reports via email involves the same steps required to export reports to Excel and PDF format. Follow steps one through four in the *Exporting reports to Excel* section. We will cover the remaining steps here.

Follow these steps to send reports via email:

1. Click on the icon that resembles an envelope, as follows:

2. Click on the **Email** option, as follows:

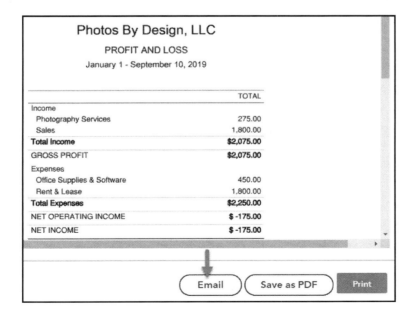

3. The following window will be displayed:

The following is a brief description of the fields that need to be completed:

- **To**: Enter the email address of each recipient in this field. You can enter multiple email addresses by putting a comma (,) in between each one.
- **CC**: Enter the email address for each recipient that needs to receive a carbon copy of the report. To enter multiple email addresses, put a comma (,) in between each email address.
- **Subject**: This field will automatically populate with the name of the report. You can make changes to this field.
- **Body**: This field will automatically populate with a standard message. You can customize the email message to fit your needs.
- **Report**: The report you are emailing will be attached as a PDF document.
- **Send**: After completing all the fields, click the **Send** button to email the report.

Emailing reports can be an easy and secure way to share data with your accountant and stakeholders in your business. The reports are attached in a PDF format so they cannot be manipulated.

Summary

As promised, we have introduced you to the report center and covered all of the different types of reports available at your fingertips. You have learned how to run reports, edit the data on reports, and save your changes. We have shown you how to share your data by printing a hard copy, exporting the information to Excel, saving to a PDF format, and emailing directly from QuickBooks. This will help you to safely and securely share information on a need-to-know basis instead of giving access to your company data. We have covered all of the objectives for this chapter and are ready to move onto the next chapter.

In the next chapter, we will dive deeper into business overview reports. As discussed at the beginning of this chapter, business overview reports give you an insight into the overall health of your business. The profit and loss statement, balance sheet report, statement of cash flows, and the budgeting/forecasting tools available are included in business overview reports.

10
Business Overview Reports

In Chapter 9, *Report Center Overview*, we explained how to navigate the report center, the reports that are available based on your QBO subscription level, and how to customize reports to meet your business needs. In this chapter, we will discuss the three primary reports that provide a good overview of your business: profit and loss statements, balance sheet reports, and statements of cash flows. We will explain what information is included in each report, how to customize it, and how to generate the report. Plus, we will show you how to create a budget from scratch so that you can keep track of your income and expenses in relation to the set budget for the year. This information will go a long way in helping you make decisions about your business.

The following topics will be covered in this chapter:

- Generating balance sheet reports
- Understanding the statements of cash flows
- Creating a budget

Understanding profit and loss statements

The profit and loss statement, also referred to as the income statement, will show you how profitable a business is for a period of time. This report summarizes all the income and expenses that have been incurred by a business for a specific period of time. The difference between income and expenses is shown on the report as either net profit (income exceeds expenses) or net loss (expenses exceed income). Like most reports, you can customize the profit and loss statement to meet your business needs. We will show you how to customize and generate the report in this section.

Follow these steps to customize and generate a profit and loss statement:

1. Navigate to **Reports** in the left menu bar, as shown in the following screenshot:

2. Scroll down to the business overview section and select **Profit and Loss**, as shown in the following screenshot:

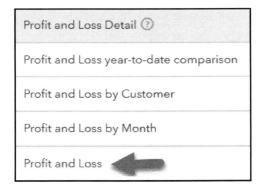

As you can see, there are several different types of profit and loss reports you can run in QuickBooks Online. The profit and loss detail report, profit and loss year-to-date comparison, profit and loss by customer, and profit and loss by month are preset custom reports.

3. You can customize the date range, columns to display, and accounting period, as shown in the following screenshot:

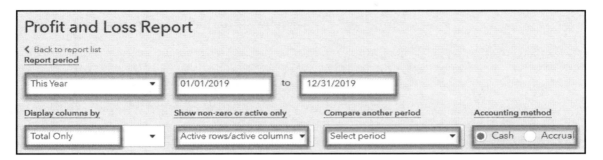

Brief descriptions of the basic customization options for a profit and loss report are as follows:

- **Report period**: From the drop-down menu, you can choose a preselected time period (such as this year) and the from/to date fields will automatically populate for you. The other option is to type directly into the from/to date fields.
- **Display columns by**: There are a number of options you can choose from when it comes to how to display columns. From the dropdown, you can select days, weeks, months, quarters, years, customers, vendors, employees, and product or service.
- **Show non-zero or active only**: This field allows you to determine whether you want columns and rows to display for all active accounts, regardless of whether they have activity or a zero amount. You can also choose non-zero, which means only accounts that have an amount will show up on the report.
- **Compare another period**: As we discussed in `Chapter 9`, *Report Center Overview*, you can compare your data to a previous period by making a selection from the dropdown.
- **Accounting method**: As we discussed in `Chapter 9`, *Report Center Overview*, you can choose the accounting method you would like to run the report for, that is, cash or accrual. You can learn more about the cash and accrual methods in `Chapter 1`, *Getting Started with QuickBooks Online*.

Additional customizations can be made by using number formatting, selecting rows/columns, using filters, and editing header and footer information. Refer to `Chapter 9`, *Report Center Overview*, for step-by-step instructions on how to customize reports in QuickBooks Online.

The following is a snapshot of a sample profit and loss report that's been generated in QuickBooks Online:

Photos By Design, LLC	
PROFIT AND LOSS	
January - December 2019	
	TOTAL
Income	
Photography Services	275.00
Sales	6,800.00
Total Income	**$7,075.00**
GROSS PROFIT	**$7,075.00**
Expenses	
Car & Truck	45.00
Meals & Entertainment	80.00
Office Supplies & Software	450.00
Rent & Lease	1,800.00
Utilities	
Telephone Expense	120.00
Total Utilities	**120.00**
Total Expenses	**$2,495.00**
NET OPERATING INCOME	**$4,580.00**
NET INCOME	**$4,580.00**

In the sample profit and loss report, **Photos By Design** has a total income of **$7,075** and expenses totaling **$2,495**, which yields a net profit of **$4,580** for the period **January 1 to December 31, 2019**. Next, we will show you how to run a balance sheet report, which shows all assets, liabilities, and equity for a business.

Generating balance sheet reports

A balance sheet report summarizes the assets, liabilities, and owner's equity for a business at any point in time. This report allows you to assess the liquidity of a business, which is important to potential investors and creditors. As with most reports, you can customize the balance sheet report to meet your business needs. We will show you how to generate the report and customize it in this section.

Follow these steps to customize and generate a balance sheet report:

1. Navigate to **Reports** in the left menu bar, as shown in the following screenshot:

2. Scroll down to the business overview section and select **Balance Sheet**, as shown in the following screenshot:

As you can see, there are several different types of balance sheet reports you can run in QuickBooks Online. The balance sheet comparison report, balance sheet detail report, and the balance sheet summary report are preset custom reports.

3. You can customize the date range, columns to display, and accounting period, as shown in the following screenshot:

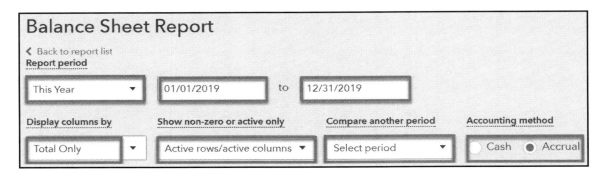

A brief description of the basic customization options for a profit and loss report are as follows:

- **Report period**: From the drop-down menu, you can choose a preselected time period (such as this year) and the from/to date fields will automatically populate for you. The other option is to type directly into the from/to date fields.
- **Display columns by**: There are a number of options you can choose when it comes to how to display columns. From the dropdown, you can select days, weeks, months, quarters, years, customers, vendors, employees, and product or service.
- **Show non-zero or active only**: This field allows you to determine whether you want columns and rows to display for all active accounts, regardless of whether they have activity or a zero amount. You can also choose non-zero, which means only accounts that have an amount will show up on the report.
- **Compare another period**: As we discussed in Chapter 9, *Report Center Overview*, you can compare your data to a previous period by making a selection from the dropdown.
- **Accounting method**: As we discussed in Chapter 9, *Report Center Overview*, you can choose the accounting method you would like to run the report for, that is, cash or accrual. You can learn more about the cash and accrual methods in Chapter 1, *Getting Started with QuickBooks Online*.

Additional customizations can be made by using number formatting, selecting rows/columns, using filters, and editing header and footer information. Refer to Chapter 9, *Report Center Overview*, for step-by-step instructions on how to customize reports in QuickBooks Online.

The following is a snapshot of a sample balance sheet report that's been generated in QuickBooks Online:

Photos By Design, LLC
BALANCE SHEET
As of December 31, 2019

	TOTAL
ASSETS	
Current Assets	
Bank Accounts	
Business Checking	6,530.00
Total Bank Accounts	**$6,530.00**
Accounts Receivable	
Accounts Receivable (A/R)	5,350.00
Total Accounts Receivable	**$5,350.00**
Total Current Assets	**$11,880.00**
TOTAL ASSETS	**$11,880.00**
LIABILITIES AND EQUITY	
Liabilities	
Current Liabilities	
Accounts Payable	
Accounts Payable (A/P)	1,800.00
Total Accounts Payable	**$1,800.00**
Credit Cards	
Bank of the U.S.A	1,200.00
Total Credit Cards	**$1,200.00**
Total Current Liabilities	**$3,000.00**
Total Liabilities	**$3,000.00**
Equity	
Opening Balance Equity	4,300.00
Retained Earnings	
Net Income	4,580.00
Total Equity	**$8,880.00**
TOTAL LIABILITIES AND EQUITY	**$11,880.00**

In the sample balance sheet report (shown in the preceding screenshot), **Photos By Design** has total assets of **$11,880**, liabilities totaling **$3,000**, and total equity of **$8,880** for the period **January 1 to December 31, 2019**. Next, we will show you how to run a statement of cash flows report, which gives you insight into the cash flow of a business.

Understanding the statement of cash flows

The statement of cash flows is a detailed report that shows the cash coming in and going out of your business for a period of time. It categorizes cash flow into three categories: operating, investing, and financing activities. Similar to the profit and loss and balance sheet reports, you can customize the statement of cash flows to meet your business needs. We will show you how to generate the report and customize it in this section.

Follow these steps to customize and generate a statement of cash flows report:

1. Navigate to **Reports** in the left menu bar, as shown in the following screenshot:

2. Scroll down to the business overview section and select **Statement of Cash Flows**, as shown in the following screenshot:

3. You can customize the date range and columns to display, as shown in the following screenshot:

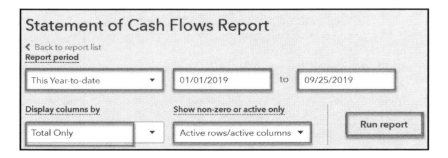

Brief descriptions of the basic customization options for a statement of cash flows report are as follows:

- **Report period**: From the drop-down menu, you can choose a preselected time period (such as this year) and the from/to date fields will automatically populate for you. The other option is to type directly into the from/to date fields.

- **Display columns by**: There are a number of options you can choose from when it comes to how to display columns. From the dropdown, you can select days, weeks, months, quarters, years, customers, vendors, employees, and product or service.

- **Show non-zero or active only**: This field allows you to determine whether you want columns and rows to display for all active accounts, regardless of whether they have activity or a zero amount. You can also choose non-zero, which means only accounts that have an amount will show up on the report.

After making your selections, click the **Run report** button. A statement of cash flows similar to the following will be displayed on your screen:

Photos By Design, LLC

STATEMENT OF CASH FLOWS

January - December 2019

	TOTAL
OPERATING ACTIVITIES	
Net Income	1,642.46
Adjustments to reconcile Net Income to Net Cash provided by operations:	
Accounts Receivable (A/R)	-5,281.52
Inventory Asset	-596.25
Accounts Payable (A/P)	1,602.67
Mastercard	157.72
Arizona Dept. of Revenue Payable	0.00
Board of Equalization Payable	370.94
Loan Payable	4,000.00
Total Adjustments to reconcile Net Income to Net Cash provided by operations:	253.56
Net cash provided by operating activities	**$1,896.02**
INVESTING ACTIVITIES	
Truck:Original Cost	-13,495.00
Net cash provided by investing activities	**$ -13,495.00**
FINANCING ACTIVITIES	
Notes Payable	25,000.00
Opening Balance Equity	-9,337.50
Net cash provided by financing activities	**$15,662.50**
NET CASH INCREASE FOR PERIOD	**$4,063.52**
CASH AT END OF PERIOD	**$4,063.52**

In the sample **STATEMENT OF CASH FLOWS** report (shown in the preceding screenshot), **Photos By Design** has a net cash inflow of **$1,896.02** from operating activities, a net cash outflow of **$13,495**, and a net cash inflow of **$15,662.50** for the period **January 1 to December 31, 2019**. Next, we will show you how to create a budget from scratch.

Creating a budget

After you've been in business for a year or two, you may want to take advantage of tools that will help you strategize and plan for the future. You can create a budget in QuickBooks Online from scratch or using existing data from the previous year. When you create a budget, you can keep track of your actual income and expenses to see if you are coming in over or under budget. QuickBooks allows you to create budgets for all income and expense accounts. You can also create a budget for specific customers. We will show you how to create a budget from scratch in this section.

Follow these steps to create a budget:

1. Click on the gear icon and select **Budgeting,** as shown in the following screenshot:

2. The following screen will be displayed; click on the **Add Budget** button:

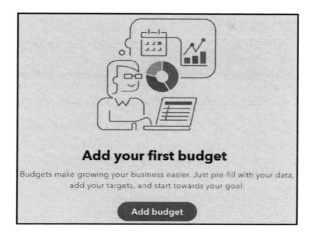

Add your first budget

Budgets make growing your business easier. Just pre-fill with your data, add your targets, and start towards your goal.

Add budget

3. On the next screen, you will need to complete the header information for the new budget:

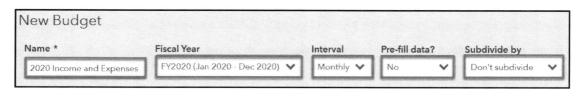

New Budget

Name *	Fiscal Year	Interval	Pre-fill data?	Subdivide by
2020 Income and Expenses	FY2020 (Jan 2020 - Dec 2020) ✔	Monthly ✔	No ✔	Don't subdivide ✔

Brief explanations of the information included in the header screen is as follows:

- **Name**: Type the name of the budget into this field. This will generally include the fiscal year, along with a brief description.
- **Fiscal Year**: Select the fiscal year the budget is for (for example, **Jan 2020 - Dec 2020**).
- **Interval**: Select the interval you would like to use from the dropdown. You can select monthly, quarterly, or yearly.
- **Pre-fill data**: You can choose to import data from QuickBooks for the current year or previous year (and then make adjustments if needed). Otherwise, choose **No** if you prefer to manually enter the budget.
- **Subdivide by**: If this budget is going to be by the customer, choose a **customer** from the dropdown. Otherwise, leave it as **Don't subdivide**.

After completing the header information, proceed to the next screen to enter the budgeted amount for all income and expense accounts. Once you have completed the budget template, it will resemble what's shown in the following screenshot:

ACCOUNTS	JAN	FEB	MAR	APR	MAY	JUN	JUL	AUG	SEP	OCT	NOV	DEC	TOTAL
▾ INCOME													
Billable Expense Income													
Design income	8,500.00	8,500.00	8,500.00	8,500.00	8,500.00	8,500.00	8,500.00	8,500.00	8,500.00	8,500.00	8,500.00	8,500.00	102,0...
Discounts given													
Fees Billed													
▾ Landscaping Services	3,500.00	3,500.00	3,500.00	3,500.00	3,500.00	3,500.00	3,500.00	3,500.00	3,500.00	3,500.00	3,500.00	3,500.00	42,00...
▸ Job Materials	5050.00	5050.00	5050.00	5050.00	5050.00	5050.00	5050.00	5050.00	5050.00	5050.00	5050.00	5050.00	60600...
▸ Labor	3000.00	3000.00	3000.00	3000.00	3000.00	3000.00	3000.00	3000.00	3000.00	3000.00	3000.00	3000.00	36000...
Total Landscaping Services	11,55...	11,55...	11,55...	11,55...	11,55...	11,55...	11,55...	11,55...	11,55...	11,55...	11,55...	11,55...	138,6...
Other Income													
Pest Control Services	275.00	275.00	275.00	275.00	275.00	275.00	275.00	275.00	275.00	275.00	275.00	275.00	3,300.00

There are two reports that you can run to review and manage your budget: a budget overview report and a budget versus actuals report.

A brief description of the information you will find on both reports is as follows:

- **Budget Overview Report**: After entering your budget, you can run this report to review the budget to ensure it is accurate. If changes are required, you can go back into the budget template to make the necessary changes. Like most reports in QBO, you can export the budget overview report to Excel or PDF. You can also email the budget overview report directly from QuickBooks.
- **Budget versus Actuals Report**: The budget versus actuals report includes side-by-side columns: one for the budgeted amount and one for the actuals as of a specific time period. The difference between the budget and the actuals will appear in a variance column. This information can help you determine the areas where you are within your budget or over budget so that you can make any necessary adjustments. Like the budget overview report, you can export the budget versus actuals report to Excel or PDF. Plus, you can email the report directly from QuickBooks.

Summary

All of the objectives for this chapter have been met. In this chapter, we explained the information you can find on the three primary financial reports: profit and loss, balance sheet, and statement of cash flows. We also showed you how to customize the reports and generate them. In addition, we showed you how to create a budget from scratch and run budget reports.

In the next chapter, we will show you what reports are available in QBO to help you stay on top of customers and sales.

11
Customer Sales Reports in QuickBooks Online

In the last chapter, we covered how to customize and generate key business overview reports, which gave you an insight into your entire business. In this chapter, we will focus on reports that will give you an insight into your customers and sales. There are four primary reports we will discuss in this chapter: accounts receivable aging reports, open invoices reports, sales by customer reports, and sales by product/services reports. In each section, we will discuss the information you will find on each report, how to customize the reports, and how to generate each report. Reviewing these reports on a consistent basis will give you an insight into who owes you money, who your best customer is, and which products and services are selling the most. Having access to this information will help you to make informed business decisions.

The following topics will be covered in this chapter:

- Accounts receivable aging report
- Generating an open invoices report
- Generating a sales by customer report
- Generating a sales by product/service report

Accounts receivable aging report

The accounts receivable aging report, also referred to as the A/R aging report, categorizes unpaid customer invoices into groups, based on the number of days they are past due. In general, there are five main categories (current, 1-30 days, 31-60 days, 61-90 days, and 91 and over). QuickBooks calculates the number of days they are past due, based on the invoice date. Business owners should review this report on a weekly basis and use it to follow up on invoices that are past due.

Observe the following steps to generate A/R aging report:

1. Navigate to **Reports** from the left menu bar, as indicated in the following screenshot:

2. Scroll down to the **Who owes you** section, and select **Accounts receivable aging summary**, as indicated in the following screenshot:

Notice there is an **Accounts receivable aging summary** and an **Accounts receivable aging detail** report. The main difference between the reports is that the detail report includes information about each outstanding invoice for all customers. This includes the invoice number, invoice date, due date, and invoice amount. The A/R summary report includes one total for each customer for each of the categories that are applicable (for example, current, 1-30, 31-60 days, and so on).

You can customize the reporting period, columns, aging method, days per aging period, and number of periods for the A/R aging report, as indicated in the following screenshot:

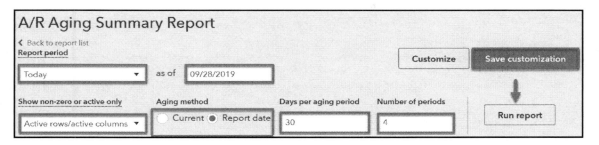

Here is a brief explanation of the basic customization features available for the A/R aging report:

- **Report period**: Customize the data range as needed by selecting the reporting period from the drop-down menu. You can choose from the following: today, this week, this month, this quarter, or this year. You can also enter a specific date range by selecting **Custom** from the drop-down menu.
- **Show non-zero or active only**: From the drop-down menu, you can choose to display non-zero only, which means only accounts that have activity will show up on the report. You can also choose to show all active accounts with zero activity.
- **Aging method**: You can select **Current**. This will calculate the age of the invoices as of today's date or the report date, which will use the report period to calculate the number of days an invoice is past its due date.
- **Days per aging period**: You can determine the number of days per aging period. In our example, we have 30 days per aging period: **1-30**, **31-60**, **61-90**, and **91** and over.
- **Number of periods**: You can determine the number of periods for your report. For example, in the A/R aging summary report that we will run next, there are four periods: 1-30, 31-60, 61-90, and 91 and over.

An accounts receivable summary report, similar to the one shown in the next screenshot, should display the following categories:

Photos By Design, LLC

A/R AGING SUMMARY

As of September 28, 2019

	CURRENT	1 - 30	31 - 60	61 - 90	91 AND OVER	TOTAL
Amy's Bird Sanctuary		239.00				$239.00
Bill's Windsurf Shop			85.00			$85.00
Freeman Sporting Goods	**477.50**	**4.00**	**81.00**			**$562.50**
Geeta Kalapatapu	629.10					$629.10
Jeff's Jalopies		81.00				$81.00
John Melton		450.00				$450.00
Kookies by Kathy			75.00			$75.00
Mark Cho	314.28					$314.28
Paulsen Medical Supplies	954.75					$954.75
Red Rock Diner	70.00			156.00		$226.00
Rondonuwu Fruit and Vegi	78.60					$78.60
Shara Barnett						$0.00
Barnett Design		274.50				$274.50
Total Shara Barnett		**274.50**				**$274.50**
Sonnenschein Family Store	362.07					$362.07
Sushi by Katsuyuki	80.00	80.00				$160.00
Travis Waldron	414.72					$414.72
Weiskopf Consulting	375.00					$375.00
TOTAL	**$3,756.02**	**$1,128.50**	**$241.00**	**$156.00**	**$0.00**	**$5,281.52**

In the sample, **A/R AGING SUMMARY** report (shown in the preceding screenshot), **Photos By Design** has outstanding invoices totaling **$5,281.52**. Of that total, **$3,756.02** are current, which means they are not due yet. A total of **$1,128.50** is **1-30** days past due, **$241.00** is **31-60** days past due, **$156.00** is **61-90** days past due, and no invoices are more than **90** days past due. Overall, this is a pretty decent report. More than 50% of the invoices are current. The business owner should focus on following up with those customers whose invoices appear in the **1-30**, **31-60**, and **61-90** day columns. To avoid sending a customer to collection or incurring a bad debt, I recommend you follow up on past due invoices on a weekly basis.

Now that we have learned how to generate an A/R aging report, next we will show you how to generate an open invoice report.

Generating an open invoices report

The open invoices report is a list of all unpaid customer invoices. It is very similar to the accounts receivable aging detail report, but it does not group invoices by the number of days they are past due. However, the open invoices report does include detailed information, such as customer name, invoice date, invoice number, invoice amount, transaction type, and payment terms. Like the A/R aging report, this report can help you to stay on top of the money owed to you. Next, we will walk through how to customize and generate the open invoices report.

Observe the following steps to customize and generate an open invoices report:

1. Navigate to **Reports** from the left menu bar, as indicated in the following screenshot:

2. Scroll down to the **Who owes you** section, and select **Open Invoices** report as indicated in the following screenshot:

3. Then, customize the report period and the aging method of an open invoices report, as indicated in the following screenshot:

Here is a brief explanation of the basic customizations available for an open invoices report:

- **Report period**: From the drop-down menu, select the date range you would like to run the report for. You can enter a specific date or choose one of the following: today, this week, this month, this quarter, or this year.
- **Aging method**: You can choose to calculate the age of the invoices based on the current date (the date you run the report) or based on the report date you entered into the report period.

After making your selections, click the **Run report** button to generate the report.

4. An open invoices report should look similar to the one in the following screenshot:

Photos By Design, LLC

OPEN INVOICES
As of September 28, 2019

DATE	TRANSACTION TYPE	NUM	TERMS	DUE DATE	OPEN BALANCE
Amy's Bird Sanctuary					
08/11/2019	Invoice	1021	Net 30	09/10/2019	239.00
Total for Amy's Bird Sanctuary					**$239.00**
Bill's Windsurf Shop					
07/16/2019	Invoice	1027	Net 30	08/15/2019	85.00
Total for Bill's Windsurf Shop					**$85.00**
Freeman Sporting Goods					
0969 Ocean View Road					
09/02/2019	Invoice	1036	Net 30	10/02/2019	477.50
Total for 0969 Ocean View Road					**$477.50**
55 Twin Lane					
07/16/2019	Invoice	1028	Net 30	08/15/2019	81.00
08/24/2019	Invoice	1005	Net 30	09/23/2019	4.00
Total for 55 Twin Lane					**$85.00**
Total for Freeman Sporting Goods					**$562.50**
Geeta Kalapatapu					
09/01/2019	Invoice	1033	Net 30	10/01/2019	629.10
Total for Geeta Kalapatapu					**$629.10**
Jeff's Jalopies					
08/11/2019	Invoice	1022	Net 30	09/10/2019	81.00
Total for Jeff's Jalopies					**$81.00**
John Melton					
08/08/2019	Invoice	1007	Net 30	09/07/2019	450.00
Total for John Melton					**$450.00**
Kookies by Kathy					
07/15/2019	Invoice	1016	Net 30	08/14/2019	75.00
Total for Kookies by Kathy					**$75.00**

In the sample open invoices report (shown in the preceding screenshot), **Photos By Design** has several open invoices outstanding. All customers with open (unpaid) invoices are listed along with the details of each invoice as of **September 28, 2019**. Open invoices total **$5,281.52** (not shown). This amount should equal the total of the A/R summary and detailed reports if they are generated for the same time period. Review this report on a weekly basis and use it to follow up with customers whose invoices are becoming due or past due.

Now that we know how to generate invoices, next we will show you how to generate a sales by customer report.

Generating a sales by customer report

The sales by customer report will give a business owner an insight into who their best customers are. In addition, you will gain an insight into customers who seldom make purchases, which can help you when creating a marketing campaign to increase customer sales. The sales by customer summary report includes a list of your customers and the total amount sold during the time period specified. We will show you how to customize and generate this report next.

Follow these steps to customize and generate a sales by customer report:

1. Navigate to **Reports** in the left menu bar, as indicated in the following screenshot:

2. Scroll down to the sales and customer section, and select the **Sales by Customer Summary** report as indicated in the following screenshot:

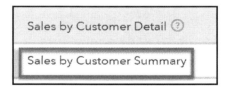

 Similar to the A/R aging report, the sales by customer report also has a sales by customer detail report. The primary difference between the two reports is that the detail report will display specific invoice information, such as the invoice date, invoice number, and invoice amount. The summary report does not include this level of detail and is more ideal for a high-level overview.

You can customize the report period, columns displayed, non-zero rows, compare the current data to a previous period, and select the accounting method to use for the sales by customer summary report, as shown in the following screenshot:

Here is a brief explanation of the basic customizations available for the sales by customer summary report:

- **Report period**: Select the time period to run the report for. You can enter a specific date range or choose from the following: this week, this month, this quarter, or this year.
- **Display columns by**: Choose how you want the columns to be displayed. From the dropdown, you can choose from the following: total, days, weeks, months, quarters, years, by customer, or by product/service.
- **Show non-zero or active only**: Select if you want to display columns and rows for all active accounts or only non-zero accounts.
- **Compare another period**: Compare the current period to a previous period by selecting one from the dropdown. The options available are: previous period, previous year, or year to date.
- **Accounting method**: Choose the account method to run the report for—cash or accrual. To learn more about cash versus accrual accounting, refer to Chapter 1, *Getting Started with QuickBooks Online*.
- **Run report**: After making your selections, click the **Run report** button to generate the report.

A sales by customer summary report, similar to the one shown in the following screenshot, should be displayed:

In the sample sales by customer summary report (shown in the preceding screenshot), the total sales for the period **January 1 to December 31, 2019** is $10,280.05. Notice that the sales for customers who have multiple jobs are broken down by job. For example, **Freeman Sporting Goods** had two jobs during this period: **Ocean View Road** for **$1,058.75**, and **Twin Lane**, with sales of **$205.00**.

Now that we know how to generate a customer sales report, next we will show you how to run a sales by product/service report, which will give you an insight into the top-selling products and services.

Generating a sales by product/service report

The sales by product/service report gives a business owner an insight into which products and services are selling the most, as well as which products and services are not selling. Similar to the sales by customer report, you can use this information to create a marketing plan that will help you to sell slow-moving products and services. This information can also help you determine whether you should add new products and services or eliminate an existing product or service. The sales by product/service report includes the quantity sold (if applicable), the total sales amount, the percentage of sales, the average price, the cost of goods sold, and the gross margin of each item sold. Next, we will show you how to customize and generate the sales by product/service report.

Follow these steps to customize and generate the sales by product/service report:

1. Navigate to **Reports** from the left menu bar, as indicated in the following screenshot:

2. Scroll down to the sales and customer section, and select the **Sales by Product/Service Summary** report, as indicated in the following screenshot:

Similar to the **A/R Aging Report** and the sales by customer report, the sales by product/service report includes a detailed version. It will break down each product or service sold, along with the date and amount for each. The summary version is ideal for a high-level overview.

3. Customize the report period, columns displayed, non-zero rows, select the accounting method to use for the sales by product/service report, and then click **Run report**:

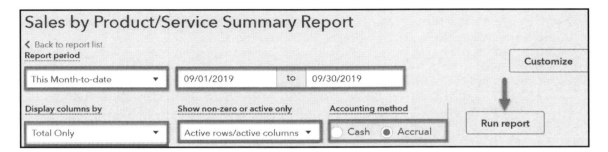

Here is a brief explanation of the fields to complete in order to generate a sales by product/service report:

- **Report period**: Select the time period to run the report for. You can enter a specific date range or choose from the following: today, this week, this month, this quarter, or this year.
- **Display columns by**: Choose how you want the columns to be displayed. From the dropdown, you can choose from the following: total, days, weeks, months, quarters, years, by the customer, or by the product/service.
- **Show non-zero or active only**: Select if you want to display columns and rows for all active accounts or only non-zero accounts.
- **Accounting method**: Choose the account method to run the report for—cash or accrual. To learn more about cash versus accrual accounting, refer to Chapter 1, *Getting Started with QuickBooks Online*.
- **Run report**: After making your selections, click the **Run Report** button to generate the report.

A sales by product/service report similar to the one shown in the following screenshot should be displayed:

Craig's Design and Landscaping Services

SALES BY PRODUCT/SERVICE SUMMARY

January - December 2019

	QUANTITY	AMOUNT	% OF SALES	AVG PRICE	COGS	GROSS MARGIN	GROSS MARGIN %
Design							
Design	30.00	2,250.00	21.70 %	75.00			
Fountains							
Concrete	10.00	122.50	1.18 %	12.25			
Pump	4.00	72.75	0.70 %	18.1875	20.00	52.75	72.51 %
Rock Fountain	9.00	2,475.00	23.87 %	275.00	375.00	2,100.00	84.85 %
Total Fountains		**2,670.25**	**25.75 %**		**395.00**		
Lighting	3.00	45.00	0.43 %	15.00			
Rocks	25.00	384.00	3.70 %	15.36			
Services	8.00	503.55	4.86 %	62.94375			
Total Design		**5,852.80**	**56.44 %**		**395.00**		
Landscaping							
Gardening	56.50	1,447.50	13.96 %	25.619469			
Installation	5.00	250.00	2.41 %	50.00			
Maintenance & Repair	1.00	50.00	0.48 %	50.00			
Sod	90.00	2,231.25	21.52 %	24.7916667			
Soil	20.00	200.00	1.93 %	10.00			
Sprinklers							
Sprinkler Heads	25.00	50.00	0.48 %	2.00			
Sprinkler Pipes	37.00	148.00	1.43 %	4.00	10.00	138.00	93.24 %
Total Sprinklers		**198.00**	**1.91 %**		**10.00**		
Trimming	2.00	30.00	0.29 %	15.00			
Total Landscaping		**4,406.75**	**42.50 %**		**10.00**		
Pest Control							
Pest Control	5.00	110.00	1.06 %	22.00			
Total Pest Control		**110.00**	**1.06 %**				
TOTAL		$10,369.55	100.00 %		$405.00		

In the preceding sample sales by product/service summary report, total sales for the period **January 1 to December 31, 2019**, are **$10,369.55** and the cost of goods sold totals **$405.00**. Design services had the highest sales of **$5,852.80**, or **56.44%** of total sales. Pest control had the lowest sales of **$110.00**, which equates to **1.06%** of overall sales. The sales by product/service report is the final report that we will cover in this chapter.

Summary

All of the objectives for this chapter have been met. Let's recap: we have shown you how to customize and generate four key reports that will give you an insight into your customers and sales. The four reports covered are accounts receivable (A/R) aging reports, open invoices reports, sales by customer summary reports, and sales by product/service reports. In the next chapter, we will show you how to customize and generate key reports that will give you an insight into your vendors and expenses.

Vendor and Expenses Reports 12

Having access to reports that will give you a detailed insight into what your expenses are, who you are paying, and the amount paid to each vendor will help you to control expenses, in order to maintain a profitable business. There are a number of reports in **QuickBooks Online (QBO)** that will give you insight into the money you owe to vendor suppliers and other creditors.

We will dive into the information you can expect to find on each report, how to customize the report, and how to generate it. We will also discuss ways you can use the report to help you manage your expenses and cash flow. I recommend you run these reports and review them on a weekly basis. Having access to this information will help you to manage your cash flow and stay on top of the money that goes out of your business.

In this chapter, we will focus on the following key reports:

- Generating an **accounts payable (A/P)** aging report
- Generating an unpaid bills report
- Generating an expenses by vendor summary report
- Generating a bill payments report

Generating an accounts payable (A/P) aging report

An accounts payable aging report, also known as an A/P aging report, groups unpaid bills based on the number of days they are outstanding. Similar to an A/R aging report, there are five main groups: current, 1-30 days, 31-60 days, 61-90 days, and 91 days and over. QuickBooks calculates the age of a bill by using the bill date. To stay on top of bills, business owners should review this report on a weekly basis, and take the necessary steps to pay bills that are nearly due. For bills becoming due, you should send a reminder email to your customers a day or two before the bill is due. For past due bills, you need to send emails out as soon as possible, requesting payment.

Follow these steps to generate an A/P aging report:

1. Navigate to **Reports** from the left menu bar, as indicated in the following screenshot:

2. Scroll down to the **What you owe** section, and select **Accounts payable aging summary**, as indicated in the following screenshot:

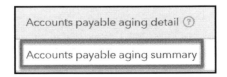

In addition to the **Accounts payable aging summary** report, there is an **Accounts payable aging detail** report. The primary difference in the two reports is that the detail report includes information about each bill for the vendor. This includes the bill date, bill number, due date, and amount due. The summary report, on the other hand, includes the open balance for each vendor, grouped by the age of the bill (current, 1-30 days, 31-60 days, 61-90 days, and 91 and over).

3. You can customize the reporting period, columns to display, aging method, days per aging period, and the number of periods for the A/P aging summary report, as indicated in the following screenshot:

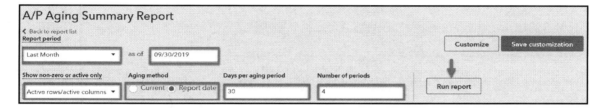

The following is a brief description of the customizable fields available for an A/P aging summary report:

- **Report period**: You can select preset dates from the drop-down menu, which includes today, this week, this month, this quarter, or this year. If you prefer a custom date range, select **Custom** from the drop-down, and manually enter the dates.

- **Show non-zero or active only**: Choose to display non-zero only, which means only accounts with activity for the report period specified will be displayed on the report.

- **Aging method**: You can choose an aging method of **Current**, or **Report date**. **Current** will calculate the age of each bill as of today's date, whereas **Report date** will use the report period to calculate the number of days a bill has remained outstanding (unpaid).

- **Days per aging period**: Customize the number of days per aging period, or use the standard 30 days per aging period.

- **Number of periods**: Similar to **Days per aging period**, you can also customize the number of periods in which to group bills. In the preceding example, we have chosen four periods (1-30, 31-60, 61-90, and 91 and over).

4. After making your selections, click the **Run report** button, and an A/P aging summary report—similar to the following one—will display:

Photos By Design, LLC

A/P AGING SUMMARY

As of September 30, 2019

	CURRENT	1 - 30	31 - 60	61 - 90	91 AND OVER	TOTAL
Brosnahan Insurance Agency		241.23				$241.23
Diego's Road Warrior Bodyshop	755.00					$755.00
Norton Lumber and Building Materials		205.00				$205.00
PG&E			86.44			$86.44
Robertson & Associates		315.00				$315.00
TOTAL	**$755.00**	**$761.23**	**$86.44**	**$0.00**	**$0.00**	**$1,602.67**

In the sample **A/P AGING SUMMARY** report (shown in the preceding screenshot), **Photos By Design** outstanding bills total **$1,602.67**. However, **$755.00** is current, which means the due date is sometime in the future. A total of **$761.23** is past due by **1-30** days, **$86.44** is past due by 31-60 days, and there are no bills past due by 61 days or more, which is great news. In order to maintain favorable credit terms with vendor suppliers, the business owner needs to make a payment, or make arrangements for bills that are past due by **1-60** days. Before contacting vendor suppliers, you need to run an unpaid bills report to see the details behind the open balances on this **A/P AGING SUMMARY** report. We will show you how to generate an unpaid bills report next.

Generating an unpaid bills report

An unpaid bills report is a list of all bills that have not been paid, as of the date range for the report. It is very similar to an A/P detail report, with the exception that it does not group invoices based on the number of days outstanding. The report includes details such as the vendor's name and contact telephone number, and a list of all unpaid bills, including amount, due date, number of days past due, and open balance. You can use this report to quickly identify bills that are past due. This will allow you to follow up with vendors, to make payment arrangements for any bills that are past due or becoming due. Let's walk through how to customize and generate an unpaid bills report.

Follow these steps to customize and generate an unpaid bills report:

1. Navigate to **Reports** from the left menu bar, as indicated in the following screenshot:

2. Scroll down to the **What you owe** section, and select **Unpaid Bills**, as indicated in the following screenshot:

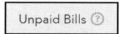

3. Customize the unpaid bills report by selecting a date range, aging method, and minimum days past due, as indicated in the following screenshot:

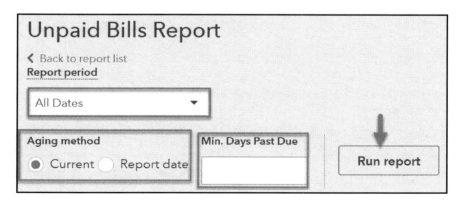

The following is a brief description of the customizable fields available for an unpaid bills report:

- **Report period**: Select the date range for which to run the report. You can manually enter a date range, or choose from the following: today, this week, this month, this quarter, or this year.
- **Aging method**: The aging method is used to calculate the number of days a bill is past its due date. You can select the **Current** option, which will use today's date, or you can select the **Report date** option. The **Report date** option will use the report period to calculate the number of days the bill remains unpaid.
- **Min. Days Past Due**: If applicable, you can enter a minimum number of days a bill is past due, or you can leave this field blank.
- **Run report**: After making your selections, click the **Run report** button to generate the unpaid bills report.

4. An unpaid bills report, similar to the following one, should be displayed:

Photos By Design, LLC 🖉

UNPAID BILLS
All Dates

DATE	TRANSACTION TYPE	NUM	DUE DATE	PAST DUE	AMOUNT	OPEN BALANCE
▼ Brosnahan Insurance Agency (650) 555-9912						
09/08/2019	Bill		09/18/2019	23	241.23	241.23
Total for Brosnahan Insurance Agency					**$241.23**	**$241.23**
▼ Diego's Road Warrior Bodyshop						
09/13/2019	Bill		10/13/2019	-2	755.00	755.00
Total for Diego's Road Warrior Bodyshop					**$755.00**	**$755.00**
▼ Norton Lumber and Building Materials (650) 363-6578						
09/15/2019	Bill		09/15/2019	26	205.00	205.00
Total for Norton Lumber and Building Materials					**$205.00**	**$205.00**
▼ PG&E (888) 555-9465						
08/01/2019	Bill		08/31/2019	41	86.44	86.44
Total for PG&E					**$86.44**	**$86.44**
▼ Robertson & Associates (650) 557-1111						
09/15/2019	Bill		09/15/2019	26	315.00	315.00
Total for Robertson & Associates					**$315.00**	**$315.00**
TOTAL					**$1,602.67**	**$1,602.67**

In the sample **UNPAID BILLS** report (shown in the preceding screenshot), **Photos By Design** has unpaid bills totaling **$1,602.67**. The oldest bill has been past due for **41** days for **PG&E**, to the amount of **$86.44**. For each vendor, the report includes the name of the vendor, their contact phone number, the bill date, the due date, the number of days past due, and the outstanding amount. To maintain good credit with your vendor suppliers, you should review this report on a weekly basis, and contact vendors to make payment arrangements. To help you stay on top of what you are spending your money on, you need to review the expenses by vendor report. We will show you how to run this report next.

Generating an expenses by vendor summary report

In order to maintain a healthy and positive bottom line, you need to be aware of what your business expenses are. An expenses by vendor summary report provides detailed information about the vendors on whom you are spending your money. This report includes a list of vendors and the total amount you have paid for a specific time period. You can use this report to gauge what your largest expenses are. Plus, you can also use the information on this report to negotiate better pricing with those suppliers from whom you purchase the most.

Follow these steps to generate an expenses by vendor summary report:

1. Navigate to **Reports** from the left menu bar, as indicated in the following screenshot:

2. Scroll down to the **Expenses and vendors** section, and select the **Expenses by Vendor Summary** report, as indicated in the following screenshot:

> Expenses by Vendor Summary

3. You can customize an expenses by vendor summary report by reporting period, columns to display, and accounting method, as indicated in the following screenshot:

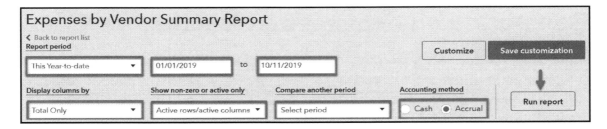

The following is a brief description of the customizable fields available for an expenses by vendor summary report:

- **Report period**: From the drop-down menu, select a reporting period, or manually enter the date range for which to run the report.
- **Display columns by**: You can format the report to display information by total only, days, weeks, months, quarters, years, customers, or vendors.
- **Show non-zero or active only**: You can choose to display non-zero only, which means only accounts with activity for the period will show up on the report.
- **Compare another period**: You can compare the current period to a previous period from the drop-down menu.
- **Accounting method**: Select the accounting method (**Cash** or **Accrual**) for which you would like to run the report.
- **Run report**: After making your selections, click the **Run report** button, to generate the report.

An expenses by vendor summary report, similar to the following one, should be displayed:

Photos By Design, LLC	
EXPENSES BY VENDOR SUMMARY	
January - December 2019	
	TOTAL
Autos R Us	34.00
Bob's Burger Joint	28.49
Books by Bessie	130.00
Brosnahan Insurance Agency	2,241.23
Cal Telephone	130.86
Chin's Gas and Oil	534.41
Diego's Road Warrior Bodyshop	755.00
Ellis Equipment Rental	112.00
Hall Properties	900.00
Hicks Hardware	620.51
Lee Advertising	74.86
Mahoney Mugs	18.08
Norton Lumber and Building Materials	103.55
Pam Seitz	75.00
PG&E	200.53
Robertson & Associates	865.00
Squeaky Kleen Car Wash	79.96
Tania's Nursery	563.11
Tim Philip Masonry	666.00
Tony Rondonuwu	100.00
TOTAL	$8,232.59

In the sample expenses by vendor summary report (shown in the preceding screenshot), total expenses for **Photos By Design** are **$8,232.59**. **Brosnahan Insurance Agency** received the highest payment of **$2,241.23**. The report gives business owners insight into who they are spending their money with. As discussed, this can be helpful when it comes to negotiating a better price for goods and services. To drill down to specific payments made to vendors, you can run a bill payments report. We will show you how to generate this report next.

Generating a bill payments report

A bill payments report includes detailed payment information about the bills you have paid. The report is broken down by the method of payment (for example, cash, credit card, or check). It includes the payment date, check number (if applicable), vendor, and the amount paid. If you want to determine the payments made for a specific time period, this report will give you the information you need.

To generate a bill payments report, follow these steps:

1. Navigate to **Reports** from the left menu bar, as indicated in the following screenshot:

2. Scroll down to the **What you owe** section, and select the **Bill Payment List**, as indicated in the following screenshot:

3. You can customize the **Report period** and determine how the report is grouped, as indicated in the following screenshot:

The following is a brief description of the customizable fields for a bill payments report:

- **Report period**: Select a preset time period, such as today, this week, this month, this quarter, or this year. You can also select **Custom**, and enter a date range.
- **Group by**: When it comes to sorting, you can group the report by account, vendor, day, week, month, quarter, or year.
- **Run report**: After making your selections, click the **Run report** button, to generate the bill payment list report.

4. A bill payment list report, similar to the following one, should be displayed:

Photos By Design, LLC

BILL PAYMENT LIST
All Dates

DATE	NUM	VENDOR	AMOUNT
Checking			
09/12/2019	1	Brosnahan Insurance Agency	-2,000.00
09/13/2019	3	Books by Bessie	-75.00
09/14/2019	6	PG&E	-114.09
08/25/2019	7	Hicks Hardware	-250.00
09/14/2019	45	Tim Philip Masonry	-666.00
06/13/2019	10	Robertson & Associates	-300.00
09/08/2019	11	Hall Properties	-900.00
Total for Checking			**$ -4,305.09**
Mastercard			
09/13/2019	1	Cal Telephone	74.36
09/15/2019	1	Cal Telephone	56.50
09/15/2019	1	Norton Lumber and Building Materials	103.55
Total for Mastercard			**$234.41**

In the sample **BILL PAYMENT LIST** report (shown in the preceding screenshot), **Photos By Design** has paid a total of **$-4,305.09** in checks and **$234.41** via Mastercard. This report includes the payment date, check number (or payment reference number), vendor, and the amount paid. You can run this report for any time period, to gain insight into payments made to all vendors. This information can help you to forecast the amount of cash you need available to meet your obligations to vendors.

Summary

In this chapter, we have provided you with information about four key reports that will help you to control your business expenses and stay on top of payments to your vendors. Our goal was to introduce you to an A/P aging report, an unpaid bills report, an expenses by vendor report, and a bill payments report. We have accomplished this goal by providing step-by-step instructions on how to customize and generate each of these reports. Now, you can stay on top of your vendor expenses by generating an A/P aging report, an unpaid bills report, an expenses by vendor report, and a bill payments report. In the next chapter, we will show you how to set up and manage your employees and contractors.

13
Managing Payroll in QuickBooks Online

Managing payroll is one of the most important aspects of your business. If not done right, it could negatively impact your employees if they are not paid the right amount. It could also result in interest and penalties if payroll taxes are not filed and paid on time. There are four main aspects of managing payroll: setting up your employees with the proper deductions and benefit elections, processing payroll by ensuring the hours paid are correct and on time, generating payroll reports to gain insight into total payroll costs, and filing payroll tax forms and making payments on time. By the end of this chapter, you will be able to set up your employees, pay your employees, generate key payroll reports, file payroll tax forms, and make payroll tax payments.

In this chapter, we will cover the following topics:

- Setting up payroll
- Running payroll
- Generating payroll reports
- Filing payroll tax forms and payments

Setting up payroll

The most important aspect of ensuring an accurate payroll is to set up the payroll properly before you run your first payroll. Setting up a payroll involves gathering information about your employees such as their names, mailing addresses, and social security numbers. As an employer, you will need a federal tax ID number and a separate bank account for payroll checks and payroll taxes. You will need to determine what benefits you will offer employees, how often you will pay employees (for example, weekly, bi-weekly, or monthly), and the payment method you will use (for example, paper check or direct deposit). In this section, we will provide you with a checklist of information you need to have handy to complete your employer profile and set up employees. Next, we will show you how to set up payroll in QuickBooks Online.

Payroll setup checklist and key documents

As discussed, the key to ensuring the accuracy of payroll checks, payroll tax forms, and payments is to ensure your payroll is set up properly. To set up a payroll, you will need to gather information from your employees. Also, you will need to have certain documents and information handy to complete the employer information section.

The following is a summarized checklist of the information required to set up your payroll:

Employee Info	Employer Info
Hire Date	Federal Tax ID (FEIN)
Form W-4: Employee Withholding info	State Employer ID Number (if applicable)
Salary or Hourly rate	Bank account information
Sick or Vacation accrual rate	Employee Benefits
Payroll Deductions and Contributions	Employee Travel Reimbursement policy
Payment Method	Other Compensation: Bonuses, commissions
Direct Deposit Authorization (if applicable)	Other Deductions: Wage Garnishment

The following is a brief explanation of the **employee** information required to set up payroll:

- **Hire Date**: This is the official start date for an employee. This information will be used to determine benefits eligibility as well as vacation and sick pay.
- **Form W-4**: This is an official form issued by the **Internal Revenue Service (IRS)** to gather employee withholding information. You can download this form from IRS.gov and include it in your employee new hire packet.

- **Salary or Hourly rate**: This is the agreed-upon salary or hourly rate for an employee.
- **Payroll Deductions and Contributions**: These are the deductions or contributions for health care, 401K, or other benefits an employee has agreed to participate in.
- **Payment Method**: Most employers will pay their employees in the form of a check or direct deposit. If the employee signs up for the direct deposit, they will need to complete a direct deposit authorization form.
- **Direct Deposit Authorization**: This form gives the employer the authority to deposit funds into an employee's bank account. Employers must keep this form on file along with other payroll information.

The following is a brief explanation of the **employer** information required to set up a payroll:

- **Federal Employer Identification Number (FEIN)**: Employers are required to have a federal tax ID number before they can process payroll for employees. This number is used by the IRS to keep track of employee and employer payroll tax payments and filings. If you don't have an FEIN, you can apply for one at `IRS.gov`.
- **State Employer Identification Number**: If you live in one of eight states that are subject to income tax, you will need to apply for a state employer identification number. Similar to the FEIN, the state employer ID number is used to keep track of payroll taxes.
- **Bank Account Information**: As discussed, you need to set up a separate bank account to keep track of payments made to employees in the form of payroll checks or direct deposits. Also, all payroll tax payments made to the IRS or your state need to be made out of this account. Since most payments are made electronically, you will need the routing number of your financial institution and full account number.

Similar to your business checking account, you will need to add the payroll bank account to your chart of accounts list in QuickBooks. Refer to `Chapter 4`, *Customizing QuickBooks for your Business*. In this chapter, we cover how to add an account to the chart of accounts list.

- **Employee Benefits**: Details regarding benefits provided to employees will need to be entered into QuickBooks. This includes the employee and employer portion of health care, 401K plans, and sick leave and vacation pay.
- **Employee Travel Reimbursement policy**: If employees travel on behalf of your business and incur expenses such as business meals, airfare, and hotel costs, you need to set up your payroll to reimburse employees for these.

A simpler way to handle employee reimbursements is to process the payments outside of payroll. This would involve setting up an employee as a vendor and writing a check to reimburse them for business expenses paid with personal funds.

- **Other Compensation**: If you pay bonuses, commissions, or make other forms of payment to employees, you will need to include this information in your payroll setup.
- **Other Deductions**: On occasion, you may receive wage garnishments for employees who owe back taxes or child support. These are court-ordered requests that you cannot ignore. Instead, you must set up the garnishment amount as a deduction for the employee. These requests will typically have an end date that is based on the total outstanding amount. Be sure to set these payments up exactly as they are outlined in the letter. If you don't, you could be subject to penalties as a result.

Setting up the payroll in QuickBooks Online

Setting up payroll in QuickBooks Online can be done in seven easy steps. First, you will navigate to the **Workers** tab and select the **Get Started** button. Next, you will select the payroll plan you wish to subscribe to. After selecting a plan, you will enter basic information for each employee, including their name, email, and hire date. The next step requires you to select a payment schedule and enter the employee's pay rate, deductions, and withholdings from their W-4 form. If the employee chooses direct deposit, you will need to have them complete a direct deposit authorization form. Repeat these steps for each employee and setup will be complete.

Follow the steps to set up payroll in QBO:

1. Click on **Workers** on the left menu bar to navigate to the **Employee Center**, as shown in the following screenshot:

2. Activate the payroll by clicking on the **Get started** button, as indicated in the following screenshot:

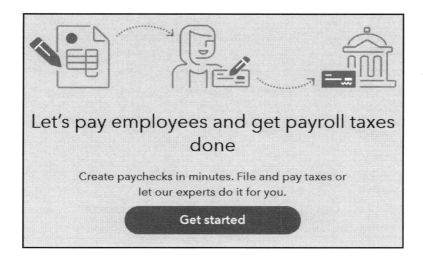

3. On the next screen, you will have the option of selecting a payroll plan, as indicated in the following screenshot:

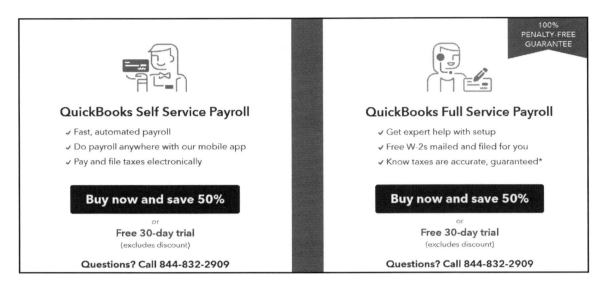

The following is a brief explanation of each QuickBooks Online payroll plan:

- **QuickBooks Self Service Payroll Plan:** This plan is ideal for employers who prefer to manage their payroll in-house. The subscription fee includes updated payroll tax tables that are used to automatically calculate payroll taxes and payroll checks for you—no manual calculation required! With this plan, you can process payroll checks, electronically make payroll tax payments, and file payroll tax forms.
- **QuickBooks Full Service Payroll Plan**: This plan is ideal for employers that prefer to outsource their payroll duties. The subscription fee includes payroll setup, processing payroll checks and direct deposit payments, completing payroll tax forms, and making payroll tax payments. Also, Intuit will process all year-end tax forms and filings such as mailing and filing W-2 forms.

4. After selecting a plan, the payroll dashboard should display on your screen, as indicated in the following screenshot:

Before you proceed to the next step, you will see a couple of questions pop up on your screen. First, you need to indicate whether you have paid employees this year. If you have, you will need to gather the year-to-date payment information for each employee so that you can enter it into QuickBooks; otherwise, the W-2 forms will be incorrect at the end of the year. Second, you will need to enter the date of your next payroll (in other words, the first payroll you plan to run in QuickBooks Online).

5. After clicking the **Get started** button (shown in the preceding screenshot), the following screen will display:

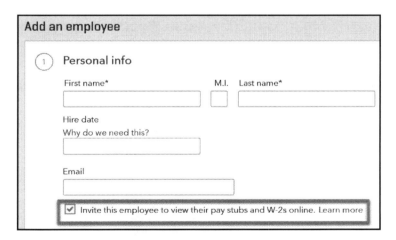

To add a new employee, enter their first and last name, hire date, and email address. Check the box under the email address to invite the employee to an online portal where they can view and print their pay stubs and W-2 forms.

6. Complete employee payroll information, as indicated in the following screenshot:

(2) **How often do you pay this employee?**

Enter a few details and we'll work out your company's payroll calendar. What is a pay schedule?

+ Create pay schedule

(3) **How much do you pay this employee?**

If your company offers additional pay types, add them here. These pay types show up when you run payroll. Learn more about pay types

Hourly ▾ $ [   ] / hour

+ Add additional pay types (like overtime, sick, and vacation pay)

(4) **Does this employee have any deductions? (Examples: retirement, health care)**

Deductions may include healthcare or retirement plans. Garnishments and loan repayments can be added here too. Learn more about deductions

No deductions (most common).

+ Add deductions

(5) **What are this employee's withholdings?**

You can find this info on this employee's W-4. What is a W-4?

+ Enter W-4 form

(6) **How do you want to pay this employee?**

In a rush? Choose paper check for now and come back to change this later. Learn about ways to pay

Direct deposit ▾

Bank account type is

◉ Checking

◯ Savings

Routing number (9 digits)

[   ]

Account number

[   ]

Confirm account number

[   ]

                                                                    1234

                                                              $ [   ]

                                        ⑆000000 16⑆ 00000052 9⑈ 1234

                                        Routing #   Account #

A brief explanation of the employee information required follows:

- **Create a pay schedule**: Create a pay schedule based on when you pay employees. You can create one pay schedule for all employees (for example, every other Friday) or multiple pay schedules—one for hourly employees and one for salary employees. Click on the Create pay schedule link in *step 2* (shown in the preceding screenshot) to get started.
- **Employee pay rate**: In *step 3*, set up the hourly rate or annual salary for an employee. You can also set up other payment types such as overtime, sick leave, and vacation. Click on the **Add additional pay types** link and follow the on-screen prompts.
- **Employee deductions**: Add all applicable employee deductions in *step 4*. This includes health benefits, 401K contributions, and wage garnishments. Click the **Add deductions** link to get started.
- **Employee withholdings**: Enter the employee withholding information from the W-4 form completed by the employee. This information will determine the amount of federal and state income taxes that will be deducted from the employee's payroll check.
- **Payment method**: From the drop-down box, select check or direct deposit as the payment method. If an employee elects a direct deposit, use the completed direct deposit authorization form discussed previously to complete the routing number and account number of the financial institution.

It's a good idea to request a copy of a voided check from employees to verify the bank routing and account number the employee has provided. If the deposit account is not a checking account, employees can request a letter from their financial institution that includes this information.

7. After entering the employee information, your screen should resemble the following screenshot:

In this section, we have shown you how to add employees and their tax deductions, tax withholdings, and payment methods. Be sure to complete *steps 1* through *7* for all employees. Once you have set up all of your employees, you are ready to run payroll. The number of payroll schedules created in *step 6* will determine how often you run payroll. If all employees get paid on the same day, you will run the payroll based on the number of times employees are paid (for example, weekly or bi-weekly). In the next section, we will show you how to run your payroll in five easy steps.

Running payroll

After setting up your employees, you are ready to run your first payroll. It's important to run payroll so that your employees are paid on time and to ensure you meet all of your payroll deadlines to the state and local tax authorities. Running payroll in QuickBooks Online can be done in five easy steps. From the **Workers** tab, you will select the **Let's go** button to start entering payroll information for the pay period. Next, you should double-check that the bank account, pay period, and pay date that appear in the header are correct. If so, proceed to enter hours worked for all hourly employees. The pay amount for salary employees will automatically populate so just review for accuracy. Review the payroll details and submit them for processing.

Follow these steps to run payroll in QuickBooks Online:

1. Click on **Workers** on the left menu bar to navigate to the **Employee Center**:

2. Click the **Let's go** button as indicated to create paychecks for employees:

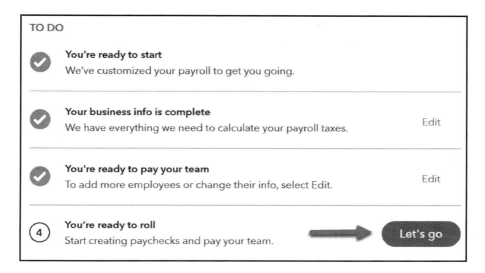

3. In the next screen, you will select employees and enter the payroll hours, as indicated in the following screenshot:

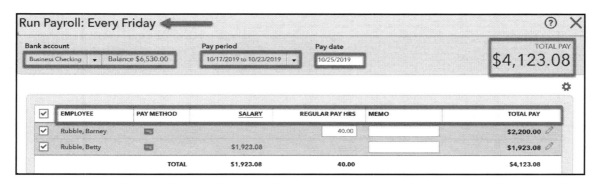

A brief explanation of the payroll processing screen follows:

- **Bank account**: From the drop-down menu, select the payroll bank account you created in the previous section of setting up your payroll. Once you select the account, the current balance will appear to the right of the account name.

- **Pay period**: The pay period field will automatically populate based on the payment schedule you created in the previous section on setting up the payroll.

- **Pay date**: This field will automatically populate based on the payroll schedule you created.
- **TOTAL PAY**: The grand total of the payroll (including wages and taxes) will appear in the upper right-hand corner of the screen.
- **EMPLOYEE**: Select all employees or specific employees to pay by putting the green checkmark in the box to the left of the employee column.
- **PAY METHOD**: A symbol representing the payment method (direct deposit or paper check) will appear in this field.
- **SALARY**: For salary employees, the salary amount for the pay period will automatically appear in this field.
- **REGULAR PAY HOURS**: For hourly employees, you will need to enter the number of hours worked for the pay period.
- **MEMO**: Enter any additional information in the memo field that you want to document regarding the payment.
- **TOTAL PAY**: This column includes the total gross pay for each employee.

4. After entering payroll hours, you can review the total payroll cost in the next screen:

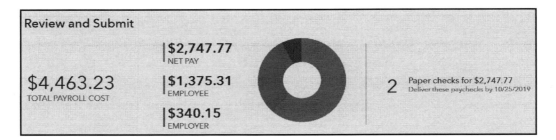

The preceding screenshot provides a high-level overview of the current payroll being processed. The total payroll cost is **$4,463.23**. This comprises employer payroll taxes of **$340.15**, employee payroll taxes of **$1,375.31**, and net pay of **$2,747.77** for two employees. Paper checks will be issued to these employees on **10/25/2019**.

5. In the next screen, you will submit payroll for processing as indicated in the following screenshot:

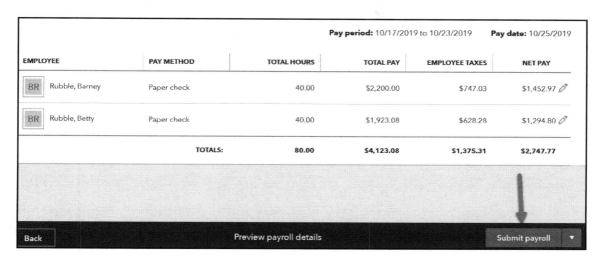

| | | | Pay period: 10/17/2019 to 10/23/2019 | | Pay date: 10/25/2019 |
EMPLOYEE	PAY METHOD	TOTAL HOURS	TOTAL PAY	EMPLOYEE TAXES	NET PAY
BR Rubble, Barney	Paper check	40.00	$2,200.00	$747.03	$1,452.97
BR Rubble, Betty	Paper check	40.00	$1,923.08	$628.28	$1,294.80
TOTALS:		80.00	$4,123.08	$1,375.31	$2,747.77

Back   Preview payroll details   Submit payroll

In the preceding screenshot, you can do a final review of each employee's payroll check. Once satisfied, you can click the **Submit payroll** button as indicated to process the payroll checks. If employees have elected direct deposit, they will be able to view their paystubs by logging into the employee portal you invited them to during the setup process. If employees elected to receive a paper check, you will follow the on-screen prompts to print payroll checks.

Now that you have learned how to properly set up employees and process payroll, it's time to learn how to generate payroll reports. QuickBooks includes several summaries and detailed reports that will give you insight into total employee costs and employer costs. We will show you how to generate payroll reports next.

Generating payroll reports

By now, you know QuickBooks Online includes a library of pre-set reports that provide business owners with insight into every aspect of their business. There are several summaries and detailed reports you can generate to gain insight into your payroll costs, payroll deductions and contributions, vacation and sick leave, and payroll taxes. These reports will help you to complete payroll tax forms and make payroll tax payments to the appropriate state and federal tax authorities.

Follow these steps to generate payroll reports:

1. Click on the **Reports** on the left menu bar as indicated in the following screenshot:

2. Scroll down to the **Payroll** section and you will see several reports, as indicated in the following screenshot:

Employee Details	☆	Payroll Tax Payments	☆
Employee Directory	☆	Payroll Tax and Wage Summary	☆
Multiple Worksites	☆	Recent/Edited Time Activities	☆
Paycheck List	☆	Retirement Plans	☆
Payroll Billing Summary	☆	Time Activities by Employee Detail	☆
Payroll Deductions/Contributions	☆	Total Pay	☆
Payroll Details	☆	Total Payroll Cost	☆
Payroll Summary by Employee	☆ ⋮	Vacation and Sick Leave	☆
Payroll Summary	☆	Workers' Compensation	☆
Payroll Tax Liability	☆		

The following is a brief description of the information you will find on the five key payroll reports:

- **Paycheck List**: This report includes a list of paychecks that have been issued. You can use this report to edit check numbers, print pay stubs, and more.
- **Payroll Deductions/Contributions**: This report details payroll deductions by an employee as well as employer contributions made for each pay period.
- **Payroll Summary by Employee**: This is a comprehensive report that includes wages, deductions, and taxes totaled by the employee or payroll period.
- **Total Payroll Cost**: This report includes all costs associated with paying employees such as total pay, net pay, deductions, and taxes.
- **Vacation and Sick Leave**: This report details the total vacation and sick pay that has been used as well as their remaining balance left.

To generate a report, simply click on the report and select the pay period you would like to see data for. Similar to other QBO reports, you can save payroll reports as PDF files or export them to Excel. Refer to `Chapter 9`, *Report Center Overview*, for step-by-step instructions on how this works. One of the key benefits of generating reports is that the information you need to file payroll tax forms and make payroll tax payments is included. In the next section, we will discuss your options for filing and making payroll tax payments.

Filing payroll tax forms and payments

Employers are required to file payroll tax forms and make payroll tax payments at both the federal and state level. The due dates will vary by the employer and are generally based on the dollar amount of the payroll and other factors specific to your business. The `IRS.gov` website is the best resource to find out what the federal requirements are. At the state level, you should contact the **Employment Development Department (EDD)** to learn what the requirements are for your state. As discussed in the payroll setup section, you will need to obtain a state employer ID number. Once you do so, you should receive information about filing and paying state payroll taxes, if applicable.

There are a few key reports that you should generate to assist you with completing payroll tax forms:

- **Payroll tax liability**: This report provides you with the details on how much payroll tax you are required to pay and how much you have already paid to state and federal tax authorities.
- **Payroll tax payments**: This report provides you with the details of all tax payments you have made.
- **Payroll tax and wage summary**: This report shows total and taxable wages that are subject to federal and province/region/state withholding.

 If you sign up for the payroll QuickBooks Full Service subscription, Intuit will file all of your tax forms and submit all payroll tax payments for you. However, if you signed up for the QuickBooks Self Service subscription, you will be responsible for filing all paperwork and making all payroll tax payments before the due date.

As discussed, it's important to file all payroll tax forms and mail payroll tax payments before they are due. Otherwise, you could be subject to hefty penalties and fines if you do not. Contact the IRS to get information about federal forms and due dates, and contact the EDD in your state for information regarding the state forms and due dates.

Summary

We have met our goal for this chapter of showing you how to manage your payroll from start to finish. To recap, you now know what information is required to set up employees and how to set them up. We covered how to enter the hours for each pay period and submit payroll for processing. You know what payroll reports are available so that you can gain insight into your total payroll costs, and finally, we discussed the importance of filing payroll tax forms and submitting payroll tax payments on time. You are now equipped to add employees, run your payroll, run payroll reports, and use this information to file your payroll tax returns.

In the next chapter, we will cover how to manage 1099 contractors. While these folks are not employees, you will need to set them up in QuickBooks to properly track payments for reporting purposes.

14
Managing 1099 Contractors in QuickBooks Online

If you hire an individual to perform services for your business and they are not an employee, they are considered an independent contractor (also known as 1099 contractors). Payments to 1099 contractors must be tracked so that you can report this information to the IRS at the end of the year. To ensure that payments are tracked properly, you will need to set up contractors in QuickBooks; add an account to post all payments to; pay contractors with a paper check, EFT, or debit/credit card; and provide a 1099 form to all the contractors who meet the threshold at the end of the year. If the total payments to a contractor equal $600 or more, you must issue a 1099 form and report this information to the Internal Revenue Service. Failure to track and report payments to 1099 contractors could lead to penalties and fines. In this chapter, we will show you how to set up 1099 contractors, how to make payments to 1099 contractors, and what to do at the end of the year to report payments to independent contractors.

In this chapter, we will cover the following topics:

- Setting up 1099 contractors
- Tracking and paying 1099 contractors
- 1099 year-end reporting

Let's get started with setting up 1099 contractors in QuickBooks Online.

Setting up 1099 contractors

It's important to set up 1099 contractors correctly in QuickBooks to ensure payments are tracked for 1099 reporting purposes. In QuickBooks, contractors are set up as vendors, which is anyone that you pay who is not an employee. To learn more about how to set up vendors, refer to `Chapter 5`, *Managing Customers, Vendors, Products, and Services*. To ensure the information you enter is accurate, request a W9 form from all your contractors. This form will include the contractor's name or the name of their company, their federal tax ID number or social security number, their business entity (for example, sole proprietor, partnership, or corporation), and their mailing address.

Follow these steps to set up a 1099 contractor in QuickBooks:

1. Navigate to the **Expenses** tab, as shown in the following screenshot:

2. A screen similar to the one shown in the following screenshot will be displayed. Ensure that you are on the **Vendors** tab:

3. Select **New Vendor**, as shown in the following screenshot:

4. The following screen will be displayed for the new vendor:

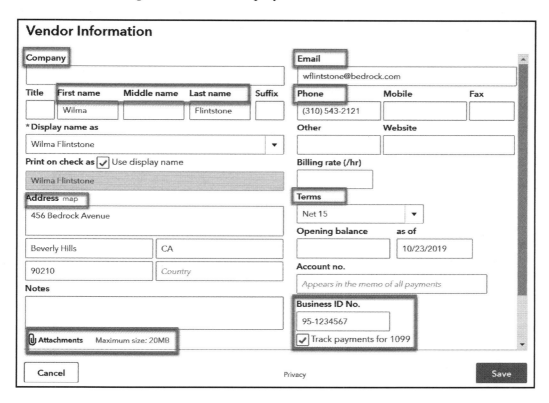

At a minimum, you should complete the fields specified in the preceding screenshot. It is also a good idea to attach the completed W9 form to the vendor record. You can do this by clicking on **Attachments**, which is located at the bottom of the screen, above the **Cancel** button.

To ensure that payments to a contractor are marked for 1099 reporting, be sure to put the checkmark in the box that appears after the business ID No. field. If you forget to do this, payments will not be tracked for 1099 reporting.

Repeat steps 1 through 4 for each 1099 contractor you pay throughout the year. Once you have added all of your contractors to QuickBooks, you are ready to make payments. We will discuss how to track and pay 1099 contractors next.

Tracking and paying 1099 contractors

The simplest way to keep track of payments to 1099 vendors is to create an account called contractor expenses. This account should be added to your chart of accounts list and used to post all 1099 payments. For more information on adding accounts to the chart of accounts, refer to `Chapter 4`, *Customizing QuickBooks for your Business*.

You can pay 1099 contractors the same way you do other vendors. You can write a check, send a wire transfer, or use your debit/credit card to make payments to contractors. Refer to `Chapter 7`, *Recording Expenses in QuickBooks Online*, to learn more about how to pay contractors.

 Payments made via debit/credit card should not be reported on a 1099 form.

Now that you know how to add independent contractors to QuickBooks, set up an account to track payments, and make payments, it's time to discuss what you will do with this information. We will discuss 1099 year-end reporting next.

1099 year-end reporting

1099 year-end reporting consists of printing and mailing 1099 forms to contractors who meet the $600 threshold and reporting this information to the IRS by January 31 of each year. This date is subject to change, so be sure to visit IRS.gov each year to confirm the due date. Similar to a W2 form for an employee, the 1099 form includes the amount you have paid to a contractor within the calendar year. This form is used by independent contractors to report their earnings for the year on their tax return. Failure to provide this information to the IRS and the contractors could result in fines and penalties.

When you are ready to generate 1099 forms, the process to do this is very simple. First, you will review the accuracy of your information and the basic contact information for each contractor. Next, you will review the payments that have been flagged as 1099 payments. If this information is correct, you can have Intuit process your 1099 forms electronically for a fee. Another option is to manually print and mail the 1099 forms yourself.

Follow these steps to learn how to do 1099 reporting:

1. Navigate to the **Expenses** tab, as shown in the following screenshot:

2. From the **Vendors** tab, click on the **Prepare 1099s** button, as shown in the following screenshot:

3. As shown in the following screenshot, review your company information to ensure it is accurate:

4. Select the box and the account you have categorized 1099 payments to, as shown in the following screenshot:

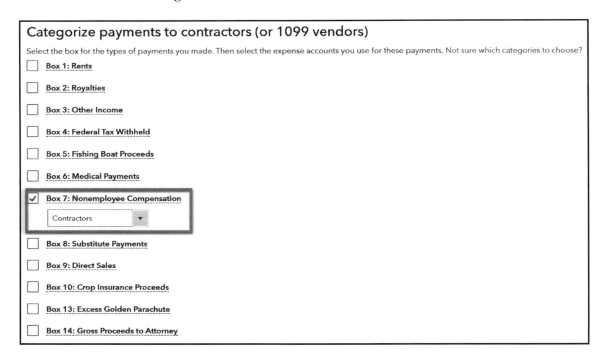

Categorize payments to contractors (or 1099 vendors)

Select the box for the types of payments you made. Then select the expense accounts you use for these payments. Not sure which categories to choose?

- ☐ **Box 1: Rents**
- ☐ **Box 2: Royalties**
- ☐ **Box 3: Other Income**
- ☐ **Box 4: Federal Tax Withheld**
- ☐ **Box 5: Fishing Boat Proceeds**
- ☐ **Box 6: Medical Payments**
- ☑ **Box 7: Nonemployee Compensation**
    - Contractors ▼
- ☐ **Box 8: Substitute Payments**
- ☐ **Box 9: Direct Sales**
- ☐ **Box 10: Crop Insurance Proceeds**
- ☐ **Box 13: Excess Golden Parachute**
- ☐ **Box 14: Gross Proceeds to Attorney**

In general, you will select **Box 7: Nonemployee Compensation** on the 1099 forms you generate for the contractors you have paid. In the dropdown after this box, select the account these payments were posted to. To learn more about which box to select, refer to the IRS instructions for Form 1099. You can find this information at IRS.gov.

5. As shown in the following screenshot, review your contractor's information to ensure it is accurate:

Review your contractors' info

Make sure your contractors' details are correct. To see which contractors meet the 1099 threshold, click **Next**.
Need to add anyone?

Add from Vendor list

CONTRACTOR NAME	ADDRESS	TAX ID	EMAIL	ACTION
Fred Flintstone	456 Bedrock Avenue Beverly Hills CA 90210	95-6789543	flintstone@bedrock.com	Edit
Wilma Flintstone	456 Bedrock Avenue Beverly Hills CA 90210	95-1234567	wflintstone@bedrock.com	Edit

You cannot print 1099 forms if the mailing address and tax ID (or social security number) is missing. You must obtain this information *prior* to printing 1099 forms.

6. A list of contractors that meet the 1099 threshold will be displayed on the next screen:

Check that the payments add up

Only those contractors you paid above the threshold (usually $600) get a 1099.
IMPORTANT: Credit card payments to contractors should be **excluded.** Why?
Need to add or edit payments?

▽ ▼ 2018 | 1099 contractors that meet threshold   **Print Information Sheet** ⚙

CONTRACTOR	BOX 7	TOTAL	EXCLUDED	ALL PAYMENTS
Fred Flintstone	$1,200.00	$1,200.00		$1,200.00
Wilma Flintstone	$600.00	$600.00		$600.00

In order to meet the 1099 threshold, a contractor must receive a payment of $600 or more within the calendar year. If a contractor was paid less than $600, you are not required to issue a 1099 form and the contractor will not show up in the preceding list.

7. Select the 1099 plan that works best for you:

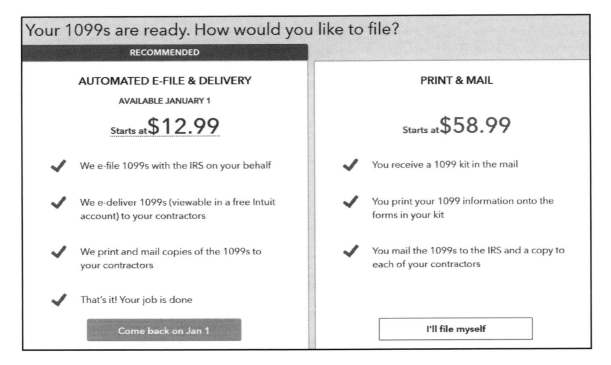

A brief explanation of the two 1099 plans you have to choose from is as follows:

- **AUTOMATED E-FILE & DELIVERY**: This plan starts at **$12.99** and is a full-service plan. Intuit will e-file 1099s, print and mail copies of the 1099s to your contractors, and give contractors access to view their 1099 form online.
- **PRINT & MAIL**: This plan starts at **$58.99** and is ideal for business owners that prefer to process their 1099 forms in-house. Intuit will mail you a 1099 kit that will include blank 1099 forms you can print on. You are responsible for mailing all 1099 forms to your contractors and sending copies to the IRS before the deadline.

To select a plan, just click the button at the bottom of the plan you want to choose and follow the on-screen prompts to complete filing your 1099 forms.

Summary

In this chapter, we discussed how to set up 1099 contractors in QuickBooks, how to track payments that have been made to 1099 contractors, the various ways you can pay 1099 contractors, and how to report and file 1099 forms at the end of the year. If you hire individuals such as an attorney or a bookkeeper to provide services to your business, you now know how to set them up in QuickBooks and track payments that are made to them throughout the year. You also know that the threshold for reporting 1099 payments is $600 in payments within a calendar year. Finally, we have shown you how to sign up for the 1099 service provided by Intuit so that you can print and mail 1099 forms.

1099 reporting is just one of many tasks that must be performed at the end of the year. In the next chapter, we will discuss other tasks that must be completed so that we can close the books for the year.

15
Closing the Books in QuickBooks Online

After you have entered all of your business transactions into QuickBooks for the year, you will need to finalize your financial statements so that you can hand them off to your accountant to file your taxes. To ensure you have recorded all business transactions for the financial period, we have included a checklist that you can follow to close your books. Closing your books will ensure that no additional transactions are entered into QuickBooks once you have finalized your financial statements. If you have a bookkeeper or an accountant that manages your books, they should ensure all of the steps have been completed. In this chapter, we will cover each item on the checklist. This includes reconciling all bank and credit card accounts, making year-end accrual adjustments (if applicable), recording fixed asset purchases made throughout the year, recording depreciation, taking a physical inventory, adjusting retained earnings, and preparing financial statements.

The chapter objectives are summarized as follows:

- Reviewing a checklist for closing your books
- Giving your accountant access to your data
- Recording journal entries

By the end of this chapter, you will know all of the tasks you need to complete in order to close your books for the year. While most small businesses close their books annually, if you close your books on a monthly or a quarterly basis, you will need to follow the steps outlined in this chapter. In the following section, we will cover the details of the checklist.

Reviewing a checklist for closing your books

As discussed, there are several steps you will need to take in order to close your books for the financial period. Depending on how often you close your books, (for example, monthly, quarterly, or annually) this will determine how often you need to complete these steps. Remember the importance of closing your books, as this will ensure that all transactions for the financial period have been recorded and that your financial statements are accurate, which is important because your accountant will use them to file your business tax return.

The following is a checklist of the steps you need to complete in order to close your books:

- Reconciling all bank and credit card accounts
- Making year-end accrual adjustments
- Reviewing new fixed asset purchases, and adding them to the chart of accounts
- Making depreciation journal entries
- Taking physical inventory, and reconciling with your books
- Adjusting retained earnings for owner/partner distributions
- Setting a closing date and password
- Preparing key financial reports

Next, we will discuss each of these eight steps in detail, starting with reconciling all bank and credit card accounts.

Reconciling all bank and credit card accounts

In Chapter 8, *Managing Downloaded Bank and Credit Card Transactions*, you learned how to reconcile your bank and credit card accounts. It's important for you to reconcile these accounts before closing the books so that you can ensure all income and expenses for the period have been recorded in QuickBooks. This will ensure your financial statements are accurate and will allow you to maximize your tax deductions.

Making year-end accrual adjustments

If you are on the accrual basis of accounting, you need to make sure all income and expenses that have been incurred for the period are recorded. As discussed in `Chapter 1`, *Getting Started with QuickBooks Online*, accrual basis accounting means that you recognize income when services have been rendered, regardless of when payment is received. The same concept is applied to expenses. For example, if you made a purchase in December but have not paid for it yet, you will need to record an adjusting journal entry before you close the books, to record the purchase. We will discuss journal entries in more detail later in this chapter.

Reviewing new fixed asset purchases, and adding them to the chart of accounts

If you purchased any fixed assets during the year, you should add these to QuickBooks. Fixed assets are subject to depreciation, which is a tax-deductible expense. Tax-deductible expenses can reduce your tax bill, so you want to make sure that you take all of the deductions to which you are entitled. If you have not recorded new fixed asset purchases, then you will not have depreciation expense recorded, which means you will miss out on what could be a significant tax deduction. It's also important to do a physical check, to ensure all of the assets on the books still exist and have not been disposed of.

To add fixed assets to QuickBooks, you will need to have the following information to hand:

- Date of purchase
- Purchase price
- Type of asset
- Make and model (if applicable)
- Year

Follow these steps to add a fixed asset to QuickBooks:

1. From the left menu bar, click on **Accounting,** as indicated in the following screenshot:

2. Select the chart of accounts and click the **New** button, as indicated in the following screenshot:

3. For a new fixed asset, complete the fields, as shown in the following screenshot:

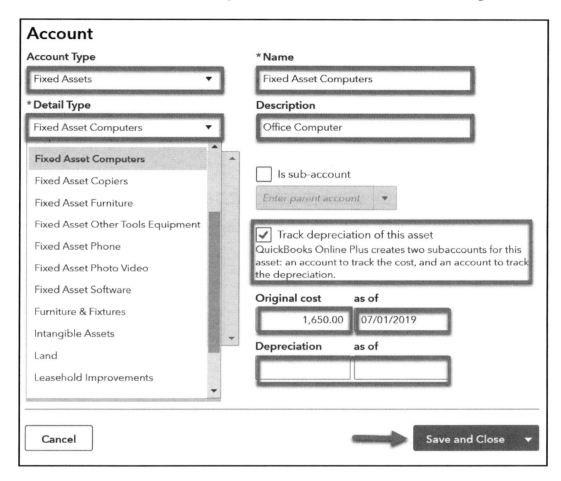

The following is a brief explanation of the fields that need to be completed for a new fixed asset:

- **Account Type**: From the drop-down menu, select **Fixed Assets**.
- **Detail Type**: From the drop-down menu, select the type of fixed asset account you need to add. The options include the following: buildings, computers, copiers, furniture, tools, equipment, telephone, software, furniture and fixtures, and vehicles.
- **Name**: Type the name of the fixed asset in this field.
- **Description**: Type a more detailed description of the fixed asset in this field.

- **Track depreciation of this asset**: By putting a checkmark in this box, you are indicating that the asset is depreciable. When saving this fixed asset, QuickBooks will automatically create an account to track the cost of the asset, and an account to track depreciation.
- **Original cost**: Enter the amount that you paid for the asset in this field.
- **as of**: Enter the date of purchase in this field.
- **Save and Close**: Click this button to add the asset to your chart of accounts list.

Be sure to complete steps 1 through 3 (previously described) for each fixed asset you have purchased during the accounting period.

Making depreciation journal entries

Depreciation is the reduction in the value of an asset due to wear and tear after it's been in service for a period of time. To reflect the reduced value, you must record the depreciation expense on your books. Depreciation is also a tax-deductible expense, which can help to reduce your overall tax liability. After adding fixed assets to QuickBooks, you need to record depreciation expense for the period. Unfortunately, QuickBooks does not compute depreciation for you. Therefore, you will need to manually calculate depreciation, or have your accountant do this for you. For more information on how to compute depreciation expense for fixed assets, check out this article: *What Depreciation is and How it Works* (refer https://fitsmallbusiness.com/what-is-depreciation-how-depreciation-works/). In the *Recording journal entries* section of this chapter, we will show you how to record journal entries in QuickBooks.

Taking physical inventory, and reconciling with your books

Reconciling inventory involves making sure that the product you have on your shelf matches what your books reflect as on-hand inventory. You should take a physical inventory count at least once a year, if not more often. After taking a physical count, any discrepancies between the books and the physical count should be recorded in QuickBooks as inventory adjustments. After recording these inventory adjustments, your books and your warehouse will be in sync.

Follow these steps to record inventory adjustments in QuickBooks:

1. Click on the Quick Create menu and select **Inventory qty adjustment** in the **Other** column, as indicated in the following screenshot:

2. Complete the fields for the inventory adjustment, as indicated in the following screenshot:

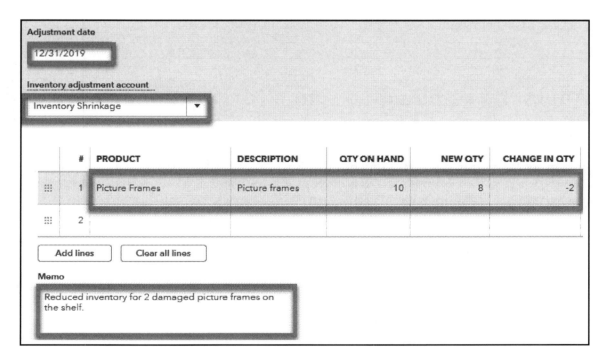

The following is a brief explanation of the fields that need to be completed in order to record an inventory adjustment:

- **Adjustment date**: Enter the effective date of the adjustment. This date should be on or before the last day of the closing period. For example, if you close your books annually, this date should be as of 12/31/xx, if you are on a calendar year.
- **Inventory adjustment account**: Inventory shrinkage is the default account that will appear in this field. However, you can click the drop-down arrow, and select a different account, if needed.
- **PRODUCT**: From the drop-down menu, select the item for which you are making an adjustment.
- **DESCRIPTION**: This field will automatically populate, based on the description in QuickBooks. You can also enter a description directly in this field.
- **QTY ON HAND**: This field will automatically populate with what you currently have recorded in QuickBooks. This field cannot be adjusted.
- **NEW QTY**: Enter the quantity, based on the physical count that was taken in this field.
- **CHANGE IN QTY**: QuickBooks automatically computes the adjustment required, by taking the difference between the **QTY ON HAND** and the **NEW QTY** entered.
- **Memo**: Enter a brief explanation as to why the adjustment was made.

Adjusting retained earnings for owner/partner distributions

Retained earnings are profits from previous accounting periods that have not been distributed to the owners. At the end of each fiscal year, QuickBooks computes your profit (or loss) into retained earnings. To distribute profits to the owners, you will need to create a journal entry to an equity account entitled owner's draw or owner distributions, and offset it to retained earnings. We will show you how to create journal entries later on in this chapter.

Setting a closing date and password

In an effort to maintain the integrity of your data, you should set a closing date and password after you have entered all transactions for the closing period. By setting a closing date, users will receive a warning message, if they attempt to enter transactions that affect the closing period. For example, if you set a closing date of 12/31/19, users will receive a warning message, if they attempt to enter any transactions dated 12/31/19 or prior.

Follow these steps to set a closing date and password in QBO:

1. Click on the gear icon, then select **Account and Settings** in the **Your Company** column, as indicated in the following screenshot:

2. Click on the **Advanced** tab, as indicated in the following screenshot:

3. The **Accounting** preferences are located at the very top, as indicated in the following screenshot:

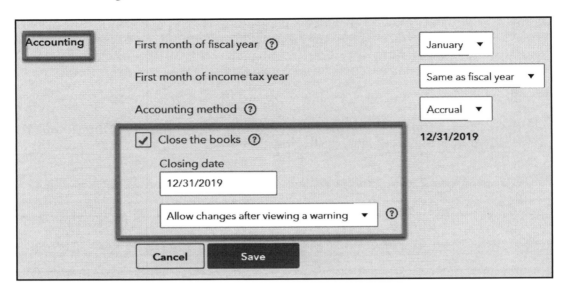

In the **Close the books** section, you can enter the closing date (that is, 12/31/19), which will give users a warning if they attempt to enter transactions dated on the closing date or prior to that date. There are two types of warning messages. The first warning message is: **Allow changes after viewing a warning**. This message will allow users to proceed with entering the transaction after they close out of the warning message. The second warning message is: **Allow changes after viewing a warning and entering a password**. This message requires users to enter a password, in order to proceed with entering transactions. To choose this option, select it from the drop-down field shown in the preceding screenshot, and enter the password you would like to use.

 Don't give the closing password to anyone who is not authorized to enter transactions after the closing date.

Preparing key financial reports

After you have completed the first seven steps in the closing checklist, you are ready to prepare financial statements. There are three primary financial statements you will need to prepare: the Trial Balance, the **Balance Sheet**, and the **Income Statement** (**Profit** and **Loss**). In Chapter 10, *Business Overview Reports*, you learned what **Balance Sheet** and **Income Statement** reports are, how to interpret the data, and how to generate these reports in QuickBooks. Your accountant or **certified public accountant** (**CPA**) will also request a **Trial Balance** report. A trial balance report lists all of the debits and credits recorded in QuickBooks for the period. If everything has been properly recorded, debits will always equal credits on this report.

Follow these steps to run a trial balance report in QuickBooks:

1. Navigate to **Reports**, as indicated in the following screenshot:

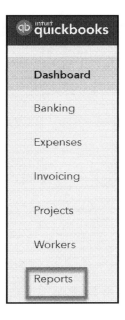

2. In the **For my accountant** section, click on **Trial Balance**, as indicated in the following screenshot:

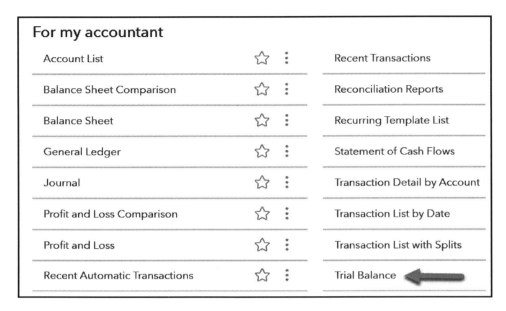

3. Select the **Report period** and **Accounting method**, as indicated in the following screenshot:

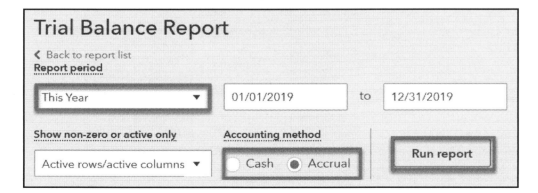

4. After you click the **Run report** button, a report similar to the one in the following screenshot will display:

Photos By Design, LLC

TRIAL BALANCE
As of December 31, 2019

	DEBIT	CREDIT
Business Checking	4,730.00	
Accounts Receivable (A/R)	5,350.00	
Inventory Asset	150.00	
Accounts Payable (A/P)		5,400.00
Bank of the U.S.A		1,200.00
Opening Balance Equity		4,450.00
Retained Earnings	1,800.00	
Photography Services		275.00
Sales		6,800.00
Car & Truck	45.00	
Meals & Entertainment	80.00	
Office Supplies & Software	450.00	
Rent & Lease	5,400.00	
Utilities:Telephone Expense	120.00	
TOTAL	**$18,125.00**	**$18,125.00**

As discussed, the total debits column should always equal the total credits column, as it does in the preceding report. If it does not, you will need to look into any discrepancies. The good news is, 99.99% of the time, this report will balance because QuickBooks does not allow you to post one-sided journals, which means that for every debit, there is always an offsetting credit to keep things in balance. If you do have a trial balance that does not balance, you should calculate the difference between the debits and credits, and then look for that amount on the report. Most likely, there is an amount in one of the columns (debit or credit) that does not appear in the other column.

To summarize, you will need to review three key financial reports before closing your books: the **Balance Sheet**, the **Income Statement** (**Profit** and **Loss**), and the **Trial Balance** report. If you have a CPA or an accountant that reviews your financials and prepares your tax return, you can give that person access to your books, so that they can run these reports without having to bother you. We will discuss giving your accountant access to your data next.

Giving your accountant access to your data

If you have an accountant or tax preparer to whom you need to give access to your data, you can create a secure user ID and password for them. All you need to do is request their email address so that you can send them an invitation to access your data.

Follow these steps to invite an accountant to access your QuickBooks data:

1. Click on the gear icon and select **Manage Users**, in the **Your Company** info column, as indicated in the following screenshot:

2. On the **Manage users** page, click on **Accounting firms**, as indicated in the following screenshot:

3. Click on the **Invite** button, as indicated in the following screenshot, to invite your accountant to access your QuickBooks data:

4. Enter the name and email address of your accountant, as indicated in the following screenshot:

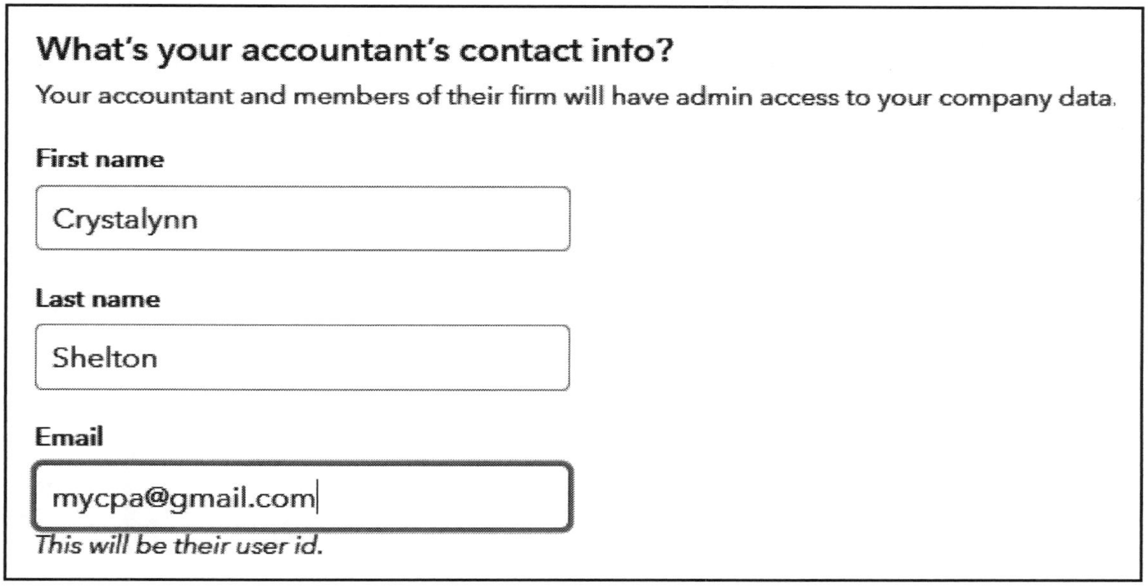

What's your accountant's contact info?

Your accountant and members of their firm will have admin access to your company data.

First name

Crystalynn

Last name

Shelton

Email

mycpa@gmail.com

This will be their user id.

Once you have entered your accountant's contact information, click the **Send** button. Your accountant will receive an email, inviting them to access your QBO account. They will need to accept the invitation and create a secure password. Their user ID will be the email address that you entered in the form (shown in the preceding screenshot). Once you have given your accountant access to your books, they can simply log in to QuickBooks, to get the information they need to prepare your taxes. Next, we will discuss recording journal entries.

Recording journal entries

A journal entry is used to adjust your books for transactions that have not been recorded throughout the accounting period. Depreciation expense for fixed assets, income and expense accruals, and adjustments to retained earnings are three examples we have discussed in this chapter. Next, we will show you how to record a journal entry in QuickBooks.

Follow these steps to record a journal entry in QuickBooks:

1. From the Quick Create menu, select **Journal entry**, as indicated in the following screenshot:

2. A screen similar to the one shown in the following screenshot will be displayed:

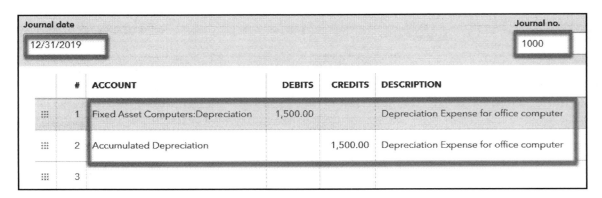

The following is a brief explanation of the fields that need to be completed to record a journal entry:

- **Journal date**: Enter the effective date of the journal in this field.
- **Journal no**: QuickBooks will automatically populate this field with the next available journal number. If this is the first journal entry you have recorded, you can enter a starting number (such as 1000), and QuickBooks will increment each journal entry number thereafter.
- **ACCOUNT**: Select the account from the drop-down menu.

- **DEBITS**: Enter the debit amount in this field.
- **CREDITS**: Enter the credit amount in this field.
- **DESCRIPTION**: Type a detailed description of the purpose of the journal entry in this field.

Be sure to record all journal entries prior to generating financial statements. If you give your CPA or accountant access to your data, they can record all of the necessary journal entries, and then generate the financial reports required to file your tax returns.

Summary

In this chapter, you have learned about the key tasks that need to be completed to close your books for the accounting period. As discussed, you need to reconcile all bank and credit card accounts, record year-end accrual adjustments (if you are on the accrual basis of accounting), add fixed asset purchases, record depreciation expenses, take physical inventory and make necessary adjustments, adjust retained earnings for distributions made to the business owners, set a closing date and password, and prepare key financial statements. As discussed, you can perform these tasks yourself, or you can give your accountant access to your QuickBooks data, to take care of this for you.

This chapter is the last one that covers the QuickBooks features most small businesses will use. In the next chapter, we will cover some additional topics, such as adding apps to QBO, managing credit card payments, and recording bad debt expenses.

16
Handling Special Transactions in QuickBooks Online

So far, we have covered the most common transactions small businesses use QuickBooks for. However, there are a few more topics that we would like to share with you. While some of these may not apply to your business when you are starting out, it's a good idea to be aware that they exist. First, we will start by using apps in QBO. Apps are a great way to help you streamline day-to-day business tasks that can be time-consuming. Next, we will show you how to record credit card payments from customers. This is an excellent way to get paid faster. Third, we will show you how to create professional-looking sales templates. If you have several expenses that you pay weekly, monthly, or quarterly, you should set them up as recurring transactions. We will also cover how to create and manage recurring transactions in this chapter. If you have a business loan or line of credit, you need to keep track of payments and the overall outstanding balances in QuickBooks. Petty cash is often used for small purchases such as stamps or lunch for the office. Due to this, we will show you how to keep track of petty cash. While you always hope it doesn't happen to you, there may come a time when you need to record a bad debt, so we will show you how to properly record bad debt expense. Finally, we will show you how to record delayed charges. Delayed charges are used to keep track of the services you have provided to customers that you will invoice at a later date.

In this chapter, we will cover the following topics:

- Using apps in QuickBooks Online
- Managing credit card payments
- Customizing sales templates
- Setting up business loans and lines of credit
- Managing petty cash
- Recording bad debt expense
- Tracking delayed charges and credits

We will begin by learning how to search for apps in the QuickBooks apps store and locate apps that are ideal for your business.

Using apps in QuickBooks Online

One of the many benefits of using cloud accounting software such as QuickBooks Online is the ability to expand the functionality of the software by connecting apps to your QBO account. The QuickBooks App Center has more than 600 apps that allow you to manage your inventory, accept online payments, pay your bills, and manage your eCommerce transactions. The companies featured in the QuickBooks app store have partnered with QuickBooks to create an app that will help you simplify tasks, streamline data entry, and sync with QuickBooks. The app store is organized into categories based on their functionality. Customer reviews are included, short video demonstrations to show you how the app works, and customer service information if you have additional questions. In this section, we will provide you with an overview of the app center, show you how to find apps that are relevant to your business needs, and how to add apps to QuickBooks Online.

Overview of the QuickBooks app center

The layout of the app center is very simple to use. You can easily search for apps, see a list of the apps you have added, and check out apps that have been recommended based on the type of business you have. Let's take a look at the layout of the app center:

1. On the left menu bar, click on **Apps** to navigate to the **App Center**, as follows:

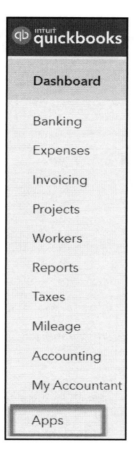

2. The **App Center** will be displayed, as shown in the following screenshot:

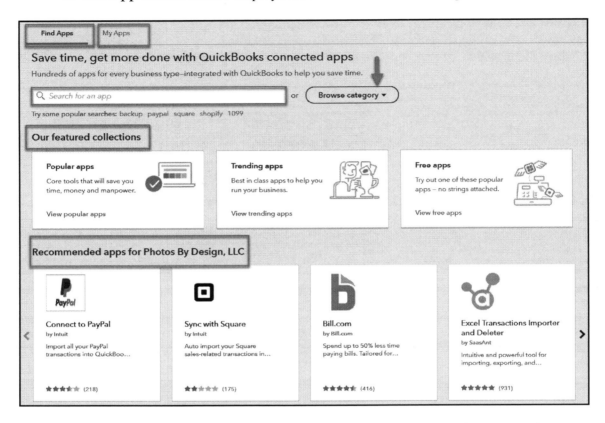

The five key areas of the QuickBooks **App Center** featured in the preceding screenshot are as follows:

- **Find Apps**: If you are looking for an app, you want to make sure that you are on this tab. You can search for apps in two ways, that is, by typing in the name of the app or browsing by category.
- **My Apps**: Click on this tab if you want to see which apps are currently connected to your QuickBooks data.

- **Search options**: If you know the name of the app you are searching for, you can simply type the name of the app into the search box shown in the preceding screenshot. However, if you don't know the name of the app and simply want to search by category, you can do so by clicking on the **Browse category** button. A few of the categories you can search by include get paid, manage workers, make payments, manage customers, manage projects, and many more.
- **Our featured collections**: This section groups apps into three types: popular, trending, and free apps. Review these collections to see what apps other businesses are using.
- **Recommended apps for Photos By Design**: This section will display a list of apps that are recommended for your business. It is generally based on the type of industry your business falls into, as well as the apps that most businesses tend to use.

If you're not sure which apps to choose, I recommend that you schedule a live demo with the company so that you can see how the app works and get your questions answered. Many companies offer a trial period of 14 days or more so that you can try it before you buy it. Like QBO, there are no contracts, so you can cancel your subscription anytime. Let's walk through an example of how to find apps for your business.

Finding apps for your business

As we mentioned previously, there are more than 600 apps in the QuickBooks App Center. While it can be overwhelming at first, you should focus on the needs of your business. There is a lot of information in the center about each app, which will save you the time you would have normally spent doing research. Let's take a look at an app to see what kind of information you can expect to find here.

Click on the **Bill.com** app. You will be greeted with the following screen:

The following is a brief description of the information you will find in the app profile:

- **Customer reviews**: Like most products, you will see a rating of the app based on customer reviews. Click on the link to see what customers are saying about the app. The more reviews an app has, the better the chance of getting a broad perspective.

- **Overview**: The **Overview** tab includes a list of the key benefits the app has, how the app works with QuickBooks Online, and additional details. Like Bill.com, most apps will include a short video to demonstrate how the app works, along with additional screenshots of the user interface, as shown at the bottom of the preceding screenshot.
- **Pricing**: Unfortunately, these apps are not free. Pricing will vary and is usually subscription-based, like QuickBooks Online. However, you will be billed by the third-party company (that is, **Bill.com**), not QuickBooks. The good news is that most apps will offer a free trial period of at least 14 days.
- **Reviews**: Read individual reviews from customers to gain insight into customer service, how well the app works, and what doesn't work well.
- **FAQs**: A list of the most frequently asked questions and answers can be found on this tab.

Once you have decided which app(s) to go with, it's easy to get started. Simply click on the **Get app now** button located on each app profile. Follow the on-screen instructions to complete the app's setup. There are several apps that allow you to accept credit card payments from customers. If you sign up for one of these apps, it will make managing credit card payments that much easier in QuickBooks. Next, we will explain how to manage credit card payments.

Managing credit card payments

In addition to cash and checks, you should accept credit cards as another form of payment. While there are fees associated with accepting credit card payments, there are several benefits. First, you can get paid faster with a credit card than waiting to receive a check in the mail. Second, if you sign up for an Intuit Payments account, you can email customers their invoice, which includes a payment link. They can click on the link, enter their payment information, and pay their invoice in a matter of minutes. Best of all, QuickBooks will mark the invoice as paid, which automatically reduces your accounts receivable balance. As we discussed in `Chapter 6`, *Recording Sales Transactions in QuickBooks Online*, you can send your customers payment reminder emails, which will include a copy of the open invoices, along with a payment link.

If you decide to go with a third-party processor, you can manually record these payments in QuickBooks. In this section, we will show you how to record credit card payments that have been received from customers via Intuit Payments and a third-party credit card processing company.

Follow these steps to record a credit card sale:

1. From the **Quick Create** menu, select **Sales receipt** from the **Customers** column, as shown in the following screenshot:

2. Fill in the fields in the sales receipt form, as shown in the following screenshot:

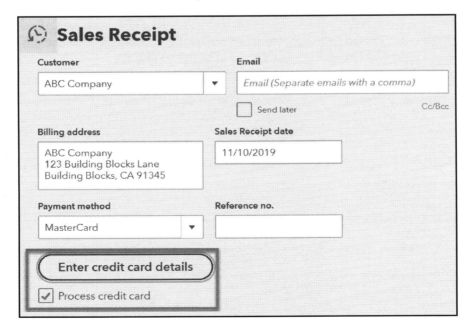

After selecting the customer from the drop-down menu, the email and billing address fields will automatically populate with the information you have on file. Next, select a payment method from the drop-down menu and click on the **Enter credit card details** button, as shown in the preceding screenshot.

The following screen will be displayed so that you can enter the required credit card information, as shown in the following screenshot:

In the preceding screenshot, the credit card number has been removed for security reasons. Be sure to complete all of the necessary fields and click the **Use this info** button to save the information.

After entering the customer's credit card information, QuickBooks will keep this information on file. You won't have to enter it again unless your customer would like to use a different payment method or the credit card expires.

This will take you back to the sales receipt form, where you can fill in the details of the services provided and the amount. When you click the **Save** button, the credit card payment will be processed and an email with the sales receipt attached will be sent to the customer.

If you don't have an Intuit Payments account, you will still be able to enter the credit card information and save it. However, you will need to process the credit card payment outside of QuickBooks using your third-party merchant company. When the payment is deposited into your bank account, you will need to match it up with the sales receipt in the online banking center. To learn more about matching transactions, read Chapter 8, *Managing Downloaded Bank and Credit Card Transactions*.

You now know the benefits of accepting credit card payments from customers and how to manage these payments in QuickBooks. You can impress your customers further by creating invoices, estimates, and sales receipts that include your company logo and branding style. We will show you how to customize sales templates next.

Customizing sales templates

QuickBooks allows you to create custom sales forms to match your brand and style. Taking the time to customize sales templates will allow you to create professional-looking forms so that your customers can easily see what they owe and make payments online in just a few minutes. You can customize invoices, estimates, and sales receipt templates. Follow these steps to learn how to customize these sales templates:

1. Click on the gear icon and select **Custom form styles** from the **Your Company** column, as shown in the following screenshot:

2. Click on the **New style** button and select a sales template to customize:

3. The following window will display four areas you can customize for sales templates:

The following is a brief explanation of the information you can customize in each of these four areas:

- **Design**: The design section allows you to create your template style and format. You will select a template design, add your company logo, add your brand colors, and choose the font size and style.
- **Content**: For content, you can select what information you would like to appear on the sales template, including your basic contact information such as business telephone number and mailing address. You can also add your website and email address to the form. In the billing section, you can determine how much detail you would like to include in the sales form. For example, an invoice should include a list of each product or service you are billing the customer for.
- **Emails**: QuickBooks allows you to email a sales form directly to customers. In this section, you can decide whether you want any details of the form to be included in the body of the email. Also, you can choose to have a PDF document attached to the email.
- **Payments**: I recommend that you sign up for a QuickBooks Payments account. By using `QuickBooks Payments`, a payment link will be included with each invoice you email to customers. Customers simply click on the link and make a payment with any major credit or debit card. They can also choose ACH, which will wire the payment from their bank account directly to your bank account.

After completing each section, save your changes. A preview of your customized sales form should be displayed, as shown in the following screenshot:

Photos By Design, LLC
P.O. Box 1915
Burbank, CA 91507
US
crystalynnshelton@att.net
www.photosbydesign

Invoice

BILL TO
Smith Co.
123 Main Street
City, CA 12345

INVOICE#	12345		
DATE	01/12/2016		
DUE DATE	02/12/2016		
TERMS	Net 30		

ACTIVITY	DESCRIPTION	QTY	RATE	AMOUNT
Item name	Description of the item	2	225.00	450.00
Item name	Description of the item	1	225.00	225.00

SUBTOTAL		675.00
TOTAL		$675.00
BALANCE DUE		**$675.00**

You can create an unlimited number of templates and make changes to them anytime. The best part is you don't have to create any templates from scratch. Now that you know how easy it is to customize sales templates, you can use one of these templates to create a recurring transaction. Next, we will show you how to create and manage recurring transactions.

Setting up business loans and lines of credit

If you take out a business loan or line of credit, you need to track the payments that have been made, as well as the outstanding balance owed in QuickBooks. This will ensure that your financial statements include the money that is owed to all creditors. If this information is not included in QuickBooks, it will not show up on your financial statements. If this information is not reported in your financial statements, you will have inaccurate reports and you could miss out on legitimate tax deductions. In this section, we will cover how to set up a business loan or line of credit, how to track payments, and how to stay on top of the outstanding balance owed.

Adding a business loan or line of credit to the chart of accounts

The first step to properly tracking loans and lines of credit in QuickBooks is to set them up on the chart of accounts. We will do this next. Follow these steps:

1. Navigate to **Accounting** and select **Chart of Accounts**, as shown in the following screenshot:

2. Click on the **New** button located to the left of **Run report**, as shown in the following screenshot:

3. Fill in the fields, shown in the following screenshot, to add a new business loan or line of credit account:

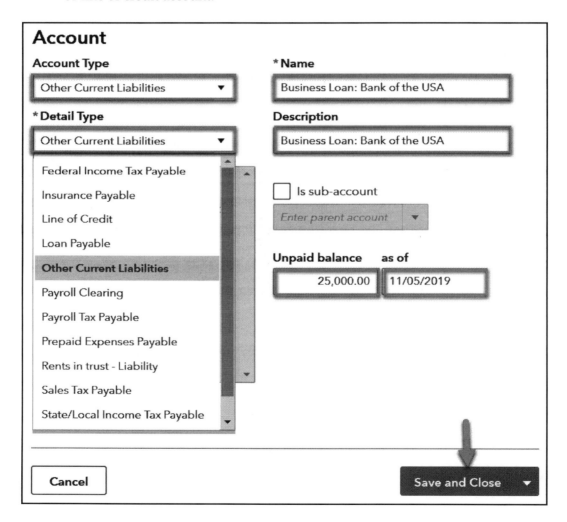

A brief description of the fields in the preceding screenshot is as follows:

- **Account Type**: Business loans and lines of credit generally fall into one of two account types: current liabilities or long-term liabilities. Current liabilities have a term of less than one year, while long-term liabilities have a term greater than one year. Select either current liabilities or long term liabilities from the drop-down menu.
- **Detail Type**: Based on your selection regarding the account type, you will see a list of options in this field. As you can see, both the line of credit and loan payable are listed. Select the detail type that best describes the account you are setting up.
- **Name**: In this field, enter the name of the account. This will generally include the type of liability (loan or line of credit) and the name of the financial institution (that is, Business Loan: Bank of the USA).
- **Description**: In this field, you can simply copy and paste the name or include a more detailed description, such as the account number of the loan or line of credit.
- **Unpaid balance**: Enter the total amount of the loan or line of credit in this field.
- **as of**: Enter the date you received the funds for the loan or access to the line of credit.
- **Save and Close**: Save and close to add the loan or line of credit account to your chart of accounts list.

If you haven't done so already, you will need to repeat these steps to add an interest paid or interest expense account to the chart of accounts list. You will track the interest portion of your payments in this account. Now, we'll cover how to make payments on a loan or line of credit.

Making payments on a loan or line of credit

In general, you can make payments on a loan or line of credit in the same manner that you pay other creditors. You can write a check or have the funds automatically deducted from your bank account. Here, we will walk through how to record a payment.

Follow these steps to make payments on a loan or line of credit:

1. Navigate to the **Quick Create** menu and select **Check** in the **Vendors** column, as shown in the following screenshot:

2. Fill in the fields for the loan payment:

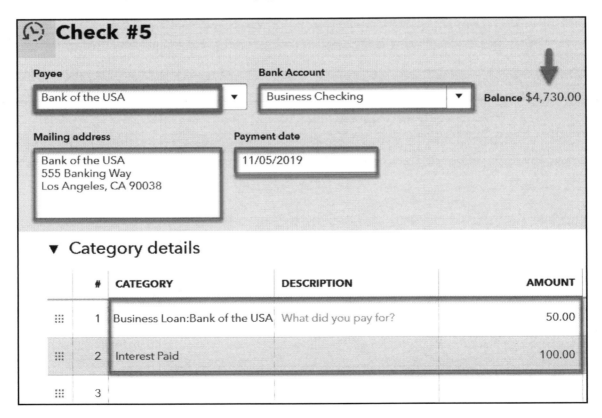

A brief description of the fields you need to complete to record a payment for a loan or line of credit is as follows:

- **Payee**: From the drop-down menu, select the payee. If you haven't added the payee to QuickBooks, you can do so here by selecting **Add new** from the drop-down menu.

- **Bank Account**: If you have more than one bank account, you need to select the bank account that you want to write the check from in the drop-down menu. When you select the bank account, the current balance will appear to the right of the field, as indicated in the preceding screenshot.

- **Mailing address**: This field will automatically populate with the address on file for the payee you've selected. If you don't have an address on file, you can type the information directly into this field. However, it's best to go to the vendor profile and add the address information there. If you type it in this field, it will not save it to the payee's profile.

- **Payment date**: Enter the check date or the date the payment was deducted from your bank account.

- **CATEGORY**: In this field, you need to select accounts that are affected by this payment. In general, that will be the loan payable account (principle) and an interest expense account. The portion of the payment that applies to the principle amount should be allocated to the loan payable account. The portion of the payment that applies to the interest should be allocated to the interest paid account.

> In order to accurately record the proper amounts for the principle and interest accounts, you may need to refer to your loan statement to see how your payment was applied. Be sure to do this so that your books match up with the financial institutions.

One final step you should do to ensure that the business loans and lines of credit on your books match your statements is to reconcile these accounts on a monthly basis. The steps to reconcile business loans and lines of credit are identical to reconciling your bank accounts. Refer to `Chapter 8`, *Managing Downloaded Bank and Credit Card Transactions*, for step-by-step instructions on reconciling.

Remember, it's important for your financial statements to be as accurate as possible. This means including all of the money that is owed to creditors, such as loans and lines of credit. In addition, in order to deduct the interest expense, you need to keep track of it in QuickBooks. If you tend to pay cash for small incidentals for the office, such as a Starbucks run for the office or stamps, you need to set up a petty cash fund to keep track of these types of expenses. Next, we will show you how to manage petty cash in QuickBooks.

Managing petty cash

Petty cash is a small amount of money that's used to cover incidentals such as postage, lunch for the office, or other items. Petty cash is generally no more than $500 and is kept under lock and key and managed by the business owner or someone designated by the owner to manage petty cash. Like all business expenses, you need to keep track of all your receipts so that you can record the expenses in QuickBooks. In this section, we will discuss how to track petty cash, record petty cash expenses, and reconcile the petty cash account. Let's get started by creating a petty cash account.

Adding a petty cash account in QuickBooks

In order to track petty cash in QuickBooks, we need to add a petty cash account to the chart of accounts.

Follow these steps to add a petty cash account:

1. Navigate to the **Accounting** section, as shown in the following screenshot:

2. Select the chart of accounts and click the **New** button, as shown in the following screenshot:

3. Fill in the new account setup window, as shown in the following screenshot:

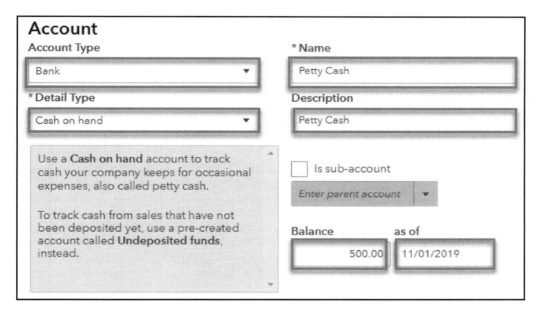

The following is a brief explanation of the information you will need to fill in:

- **Account Type**: From the drop-down menu, select the **Bank** as the account type. All petty cash accounts should be categorized as a bank account.
- **Detail Type**: From the drop-down menu, select **Cash on hand** as the detail type. All petty cash accounts should be categorized as cash on hand.
- **Name**: In this field, you can put **Petty Cash** as the name of the account and any additional details required.
- **Description**: If there is additional information that will help you identify this account, you can include it in this field.

- **Balance**: Enter the starting balance of the petty cash account in this field.

Instead of entering a starting balance in this account, you can record a transfer from a business checking account to the petty cash account in QuickBooks. In general, this is the most likely place that the cash will originate from.

- **as of**: Enter the effective date of the balance in the account. There is no need to complete this field if you don't enter a balance.

Save your changes to add the petty cash account to the chart of accounts list.

Now that you have created a petty cash account, you are ready to record the purchases that are made using petty cash. We will cover how to record petty cash transactions next.

Recording petty cash transactions

Receipts for petty cash expenditures should be kept in the same place the petty cash is kept: under lock and key. If possible, you should enter the petty cash receipts into QuickBooks on a weekly basis. If petty cash is not used that often, monthly should be sufficient.

Follow these steps to record petty cash transactions:

1. Navigate to the chart of accounts, like we did in the previous section.
2. Click on the **View register** link to the right of Petty Cash, as shown in the following screenshot:

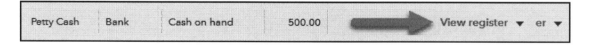

3. Click on the arrow next to **Add check** and select **Expense**, as shown in the following screenshot:

4. Fill in the remaining fields, as shown in the following screenshot:

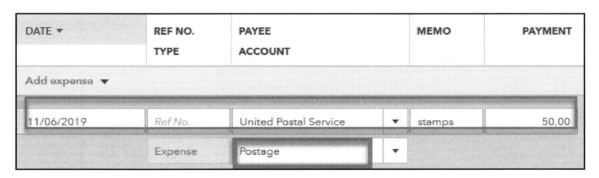

An explanation of the fields to fill in is as follows:

- **DATE**: Enter the date of purchase in this field.
- **REF NO.**: If you have a reference number such as an invoice number or account number, enter it in this field.
- **PAYEE**: Select the payee from the drop-down menu. If the payee has not been set up in QuickBooks, begin typing the name of the payee. You will see an option to add the payee to QuickBooks.

- **ACCOUNT**: Select the account the expense should be charged to from the chart of accounts drop-down menu.
- **MEMO**: Type a brief description of what was purchased in this field.
- **PAYMENT**: Enter the amount of the purchase in this field.

Be sure to click the **Save** button to record the transaction. Repeat the preceding steps to record each petty cash receipt in QuickBooks. Next, we will show you how to replenish the petty cash fund.

Replenishing petty cash

Eventually, you will get to a point where you've run out of petty cash or you don't have enough to pay for an item. Before replenishing petty cash, make sure you have entered all of the receipts for petty cash purchases that have been made thus far. Similar to a bank account, you can record a transfer in QuickBooks so that you can transfer money from a checking account to the petty cash account. Of course, to get the actual cash, you will need to make a withdrawal from your business checking account to replenish the actual funds.

To record a transfer from the business checking account to petty cash, follow these steps:

1. Navigate to the petty cash register, like you did in the previous section.
2. Click on the drop-down arrow next to **Add check** and select **Transfer**, as shown in the following screenshot:

3. Fill in the fields shown in the following screenshot to record the transfer:

DATE ▼	REF NO.	PAYEE	MEMO	PAYMENT	DEPOSIT
	TYPE	ACCOUNT			
Add transfer ▼					
12/06/2019	Ref No.	Payee ▼	Replenish Petty Cash Fund	Payment	500.00
	Transfer	Business Checking ▼			

A brief explanation of the fields you need to fill in to complete the transfer are as follows:

- **DATE**: The date the funds will be deposited into the petty cash account.
- **PAYEE**: Since you are the payee, you can leave this field blank.
- **ACCOUNT**: Select the bank account where the funds will be drawn from. In our example, it is the business checking account.
- **MEMO**: Include a brief description, such as **Replenish Petty Cash Fund.**
- **DEPOSIT**: Enter the amount that is being transferred to the petty cash account.

Once you have filled in all of these fields, save it to complete the transfer. Now that you know how to add the petty cash account to the chart of accounts, record petty cash expenses, and replenish the petty cash fund, you need to know how to ensure that it stays in balance. Like most bank accounts, this will require you to reconcile the petty cash account. We will show you how to reconcile the petty cash account next.

Reconciling petty cash

As we mentioned previously, petty cash is similar to bank and credit card accounts you track in QuickBooks. You need to ensure these accounts remain in balance. To do that, you must reconcile them. In Chapter 8, *Managing Downloaded Bank and Credit Card Transactions*, we showed you how to reconcile these accounts in QuickBooks. Refer to this chapter for step-by-step instructions on how to reconcile your petty cash account. I recommend that you reconcile your petty cash account **before** you replenish it. This will ensure that you have accounted for all the expenses that have been paid for using petty cash and that you have all the receipts to support these purchases.

While you will hope to avoid such a situation, there may come a time when a customer cannot afford to pay their outstanding balance. If this happens, you will need to write off the receivable as bad debt. We will discuss how to record bad debt expense next.

Recording bad debt expense

If you're in business long enough, there will come a time when a customer is unable or unwilling to pay you. If you use cash basis accounting, you don't need to record bad debt expense because you don't have accounts receivable. However, if you do extend credit to your customers and, after attempting to collect the payment, you become aware that you will not be able to collect a payment, you should write off the bad debt. This will ensure that your financial statements remain accurate and that revenue is not overstated. There are three steps you need to follow to write off bad debt: first, you need to add a bad debt item to the products and services list, next, you need to create a credit memo, and finally, you need to apply the credit memo to the unpaid customer invoice. We will walk you through these steps in this section.

Creating a bad debt item

The first step of recording bad debt expense is to add an item to the products and services list for tracking.

Follow these steps to create a bad debt item:

1. Click on the gear icon and select **Products and Services**, as shown in the following screenshot:

2. Select the item type, as shown in the following screenshot:

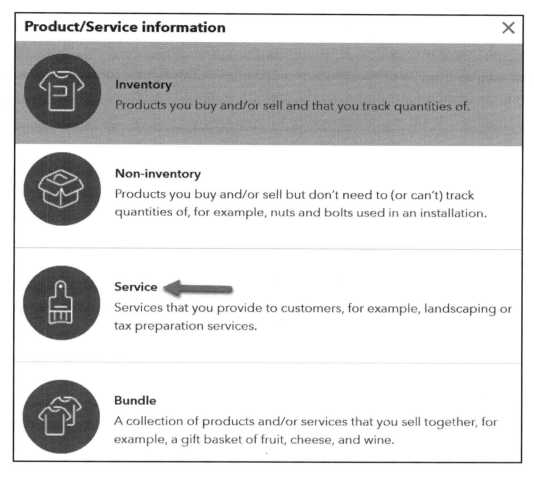

As you can see, there are four item types to choose from. **Services** is the item type we will use for bad debt expense.

3. Fill in the following fields to add bad debt to the items list:

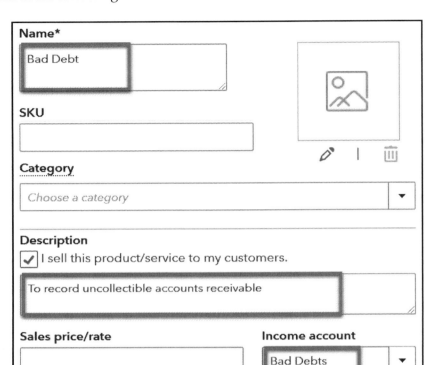

A brief description of the fields to fill in are as follows:

- **Name**: Enter Bad Debt or Bad Debt Expense in the item name field.
- **Description**: Enter a brief description of the types of transactions that will be recorded using this item.
- **Income account**: From the drop-down, select **Bad Debts**. This should be an expense account on the chart of accounts list. If you did not create this account, click on the drop-down arrow, scroll up, and select **Add new** to create the bad debt expense account.

Now that you've set up the new bad debt expense item, you can use this item to record the bad debt on a credit memo form. We will show you how to create a credit memo next.

Creating a credit memo

A credit memo is generally used to refund a customer for items that they purchased that were returned or services that were not rendered in full. After creating the credit memo, we can apply it to the unpaid customer invoice.

Follow these steps to create a credit memo:

1. Click on the **Quick Create** icon and select **Credit Memo**, as shown in the following screenshot:

2. Fill in the following fields, as shown in the following screenshot:

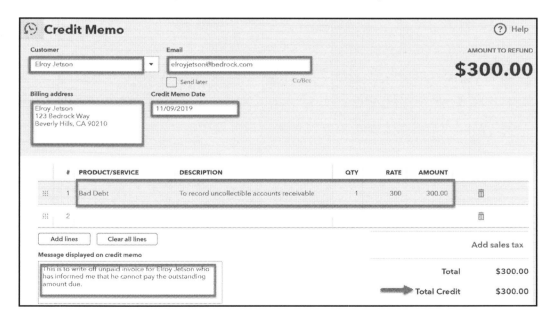

A brief explanation of the fields to fill in to complete the credit memo are as follows:

- **Customer**: Select the customer from the drop-down menu.
- **Email**: The email address that you have on file will automatically populate this field. If you don't have an email address on file, you can type one directly into this field.
- **Billing address**: The billing address you have on file will automatically populate this field. If you don't have a billing address on file, you can enter one in this field.
- **Credit Memo Date**: Select the date you would like to record this credit memo for.
- **PRODUCT/SERVICE**: Select the bad debt item you created in the previous section from the drop-down menu.
- **DESCRIPTION**: The description field should automatically populate with the description of the bad debt item.
- **QTY**: Select 1.
- **RATE**: Enter the amount of the invoice that you want to write off in this field.
- **AMOUNT**: This field will automatically populate with the amount you entered into the rate field.
- **Message**: Provide a brief explanation for the bad debt to write off in this field.

Once you've filled in all the fields in the credit memo, save it. We will show you how to apply the credit memo to the customer's open invoice next.

Applying a credit memo to an outstanding customer invoice

The final step in writing off bad debt is to remove the open invoice from accounts receivable. This is accomplished by applying the credit memo you created in the previous section to the open customer invoice.

Follow these steps to apply a credit memo to an outstanding customer invoice:

1. From the **Quick Create** menu, navigate to **Receive payment**, as shown in the following screenshot:

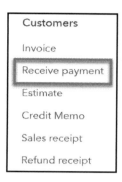

2. On the next screen, a list of unpaid invoices and open credit memos will be displayed for the selected customer:

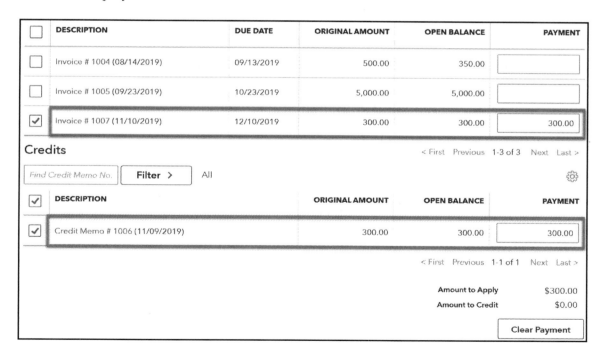

In the preceding screenshot, we have selected the invoice that needs to be written off (invoice #1007) and below that, we have selected the credit memo to apply (credit memo#1006). Save your changes to record the bad debt as being written off.

3. After saving your changes, go back to the invoice dashboard, as shown in the following screenshot:

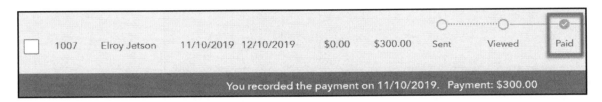

As we can see, invoice #1007 now shows the status of paid. This paid status reduces the accounts receivable balance and increases the bad debt expense so that the financial statements reflect the correct balances for these accounts. To summarize, it's important that you write off accounts as soon as they become uncollectible. This will ensure that the accounts receivable balance is not overstated.

If you provide ongoing services to customers on a weekly or bi-weekly basis but you don't want to invoice customers that often, you should consider using delayed charges. Delayed charges allow you to accumulate charges in QuickBooks (without affecting the financial statements). Once you are ready to bill a customer, you can easily transfer the delayed charges to an invoice. We will discuss delayed charges and credits in detail next.

Understanding delayed charges and credits

Delayed charges and credits are used to keep track of services that are provided to customers so that you can bill them sometime in the future. For example, if someone provides weekly pool maintenance to customers but does not want to bill them until the end of the month, delayed charges is ideal for keeping track of the services that are provided each week. These weekly services can easily be added to an invoice when it's time to bill the customer.

Follow these steps to record delayed charges:

1. Click on the **Quick create** button and select **Delayed charge**, as shown in the following screenshot:

2. Fill in the necessary fields to record the delayed charge, as shown in the following screenshot:

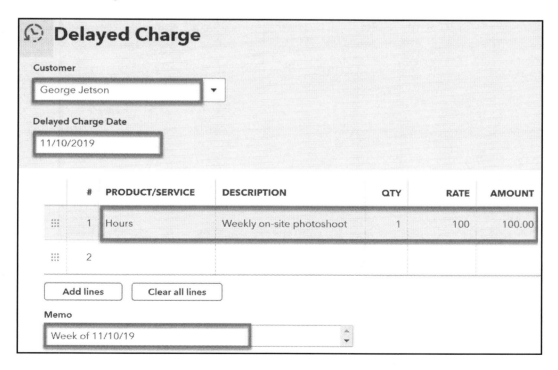

A brief description of the fields to fill in is as follows:

- **Customer**: Select the customer from the drop-down menu.
- **Delayed charge date**: Select the date the services were provided.
- **PRODUCT/SERVICE**: Select the type of service that will be provided from the drop-down menu.
- **DESCRIPTION**: This field should automatically populate with the description that was used to set up the product/service. However, you can also enter a description directly in this field.
- **QTY**: Type a quantity into this field, if applicable.
- **RATE**: Enter the total amount or the hourly rate for the service.
- **AMOUNT**: This field automatically calculates by taking the quantity and multiplying it by the rate.
- **Memo**: Enter a brief description in this field.

When you save a delayed charge, it is a non-posting transaction, which means it doesn't affect the financial statements. Next, we will show you how to add delayed charges to an invoice.

3. From the **Quick Create** menu, select **Invoice**. Select a customer from the drop-down menu and you will see a drawer open to the far-right, listing the delayed charges that haven't been billed:

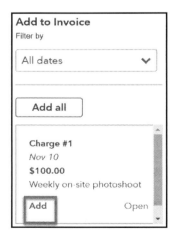

On this screen, you will click the **Add** button to add the charges to an invoice. Save the invoice to record an increase to accounts receivable and income. If you would like to review a list of unbilled charges before creating an invoice, you can do so by running an unbilled charges report. We will show you how to generate this report next.

4. Click on **Reports**, scroll to the **Who owes you** section, and select **Uninvoiced charges**, as shown in the following screenshot:

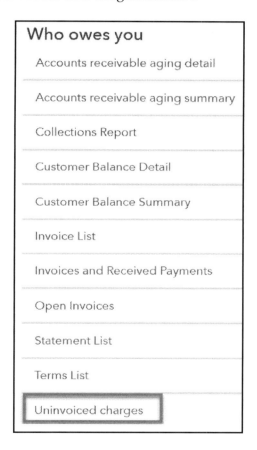

That's how delayed charges work. One last thing you need to know is that, if you need to reverse a delayed charge, you can do so by recording a delayed credit. Similar to delayed charges, navigate to the **Quick Create** menu and select **Delayed credit**. Follow the on-screen instructions to record the delayed credit.

Summary

In this chapter, you have learned how to handle many special transactions in QuickBooks Online. You may be able to take advantage of a few of these now or keep them in your back pocket for later on when you need them. To recap, you now know how to locate apps in the QuickBooks apps store and add them to QuickBooks. We have shown you how to manage credit card payments from customers and how to customize sales templates such as invoices to fit your business style and brand. For those expenses that occur often, you know how to add them to QuickBooks as recurring transactions and use them when needed. If you obtain a business loan or line of credit, you know how to set these up in QuickBooks and track payments. For those incidental purchases, you can create a petty cash account, track purchases, and reconcile the account, just like bank accounts. We also discussed the importance of recording bad debt expenses, which you now know how to record in QuickBooks to ensure your financials are accurate. Finally, you learned how to record delayed charges and credits to track services that are provided to customers that will be billed sometime in the future. Be sure to check out the *Appendix* section of this book for additional resources and materials.

Shortcuts and Test Drive

QBO keyboard shortcuts

Keyboard shortcuts help speed up navigation, which will save you time when you're using QuickBooks Online.

The following screenshot shows a list of available QBO keyboard shortcuts. To access these directly in your QBO file, press the *Ctrl + Alt + ?* keys simultaneously:

Keyboard Shortcuts

To take advantage of shortcuts, simultaneously press
[ctrl] and **[alt or option]** and one **[key from the list below]**

REGULAR PAGES - HOMEPAGE, CUSTOMERS, AND SO ON		TRANSACTION PAGES - INVOICE, EXPENSE, AND SO ON	
SHORTCUT KEY	**ACTION**	**SHORTCUT KEY**	**ACTION**
i	Invoice	x	Exit transaction view
w	Check	c	Cancel out
e	Estimate	s	Save and New
x	Expense	d	Save and Close
r	Receive payment	m	Save and Send
c	Customers	p	Print
v	Vendors		
a	Chart of Accounts		
l	Lists		
h	Help		
f	Search Transactions		
d	Focus the left menu		
? or /	This dialog		

QuickBooks Online test drive

Before signing up for a QBO subscription, you can check out the QBO test drive. The test drive account contains sample data for a fictitious company. Here, you can enter test transactions to see how QBO works. Just click on the following link (depending on your region wise) and follow the on-screen instructions.

United States: `https://qbo.intuit.com/redir/testdrive`.

United States QuickBooks Online Advanced: `https://qbo.intuit.com/redir/testdrive_us_advanced`.

Other Books You May Enjoy

If you enjoyed this book, you may be interested in these other books by Packt:

The Art of CRM
Max Fatouretchi

ISBN: 9781789538922

- Deliver CRM systems that are on time, on budget, and bring lasting value to organizations
- Build CRM that excels at operations, analytics, and collaboration
- Gather requirements effectively: identify key pain points, objectives, and functional requirements
- Develop customer insight through 360-degree client view and client profiling
- Turn customer requirements into a CRM design spec
- Architect your CRM platform
- Bring machine learning and artificial intelligence into your CRM system
- Ensure compliance with GDPR and other critical regulations
- Choose between on-premise, cloud, and hybrid hosting solutions

Learn Odoo
Greg Moss

ISBN: 9781789536898

- Configure and customize a customer relationship management system
- Set up purchasing and receiving system functionality in your Odoo environment
- Understand manufacturing operations and processes with real-world examples
- Explore Odoo's financial accounting and reporting features
- Use Odoo's featured project management application to sort tasks
- Get to grips with the basics of Odoo administration and manage multi-company operations

Leave a review - let other readers know what you think

Please share your thoughts on this book with others by leaving a review on the site that you bought it from. If you purchased the book from Amazon, please leave us an honest review on this book's Amazon page. This is vital so that other potential readers can see and use your unbiased opinion to make purchasing decisions, we can understand what our customers think about our products, and our authors can see your feedback on the title that they have worked with Packt to create. It will only take a few minutes of your time, but is valuable to other potential customers, our authors, and Packt. Thank you!

Index

Made in the USA
Coppell, TX
23 September 2020

38632395R20184